If any one person can be called the father of India's booming IT sector, it's N.R. Narayana Murthy. Murthy proved that India could compete with the world by taking on the software development work that had long been the province of the West. As one of six co-founders of Infosys and the CEO for 21 years, Murthy helped spark the outsourcing revolution that has brought billions of dollars in wealth into the Indian economy and transformed his country into the world's back office.

Time, August 15, 2007

•

NR Narayana Murthy's greatest contribution to Indian business is not the creation of Infosys, one of India's most successful companies. It is the creation of a "possibility" that people from humble backgrounds can create multi-billion dollar companies only on the basis of a vision, passion and hard work.

The Economic Times, October 27, 2007

•

His simplicity and plain-spokenness are refreshing in this era of image managers and spin doctors.

Business Today, February 17, 2013

•

Murthy knows how to combine Western-style management and accounting with the skills and drive of low-cost, highly educated Indian professionals.

Business Week, June 28, 1998

# N R NARAYANA MURTHY
## A Biography

Ritu Singh

rajpal

ISBN : 9789350641293

Ist Edition : 2013, 6th Reprint : 2017

© Rajpal & Sons

N R NARAYANA MURTHY (A Biography) by Ritu Singh

**RAJPAL & SONS**

1590, Madarsa Road, Kashmere Gate, Delhi-110006
Phone : 011-23869812, 23865483, 23867791
website : www.rajpalpublishing.com
e-mail : sales@rajpalpublishing.com
www.facebook.com/rajpalandsons

# CONTENTS

All our dreams can come true,
if we have the courage to pursue them.

— Walt Disney —

# 1

# THE SILVER JUBILEE

The man in the sober grey suit and contrasting tie stepped back a little to get a better view of the crowd —'his young ones', as he thought of them. The black hair with silver streaks was neatly combed back. Through the simple, rather studious-looking black frame of his spectacles he threw a satisfied glance at the eager gathering.

Together they had come a long way and there was still much ground to be covered. But today, the 25th anniversary of the birth of their dream, was a time for celebration. Amidst the flash of cameras, vigorous handshakes and some brotherly bear hugs, a young man approached him. From the press, unmistakably — mobile to the ear, camera around the neck, the barely visible microphone attached to his shirt.

'Congratulations, sir! Truly a grand day in the history of your organization.'

'Thank you, young man.'

'But sir, if I may ask — why are we celebrating in Mysore of all places? I mean, wouldn't Bangalore have been ideal — a bigger city, more people ...'

'There are many reasons for holding this event here. One, we wanted it to be amongst youngsters. The largest number of young people in Infosys are our trainees, who are here in Mysore. There are 4,000 of them here today, so that's the first reason. Second, we were conducting our yearly financial analysts' meet too and we had not shown them Mysore before. Third, we thought it was a good idea to give Mysore some global exposure. There were so many TV channels here yesterday; almost all the US news channels covered the NASDAQ ceremony. The name of Mysore was mentioned. Never before has it happened in the history of this city's 1,000, I don't know, 2,000 years. So we felt it's a good thing to do this here.'

'I see. Although, sir, I wouldn't say that Mysore has been ignored. I mean, ever since the Global Education Centre came up here — that itself is like a city within a city. Why has it been made so...super self-sufficient — doesn't that isolate its people from the rest of Mysore?' continued the journalist.

'No, not really, because there are 2,000 Infoscians who work on this campus but who live in the city. The only people who live on the campus are our trainees, and they need to work very hard. They have many assignments, starting from 7.30 am to 8.30 or 9 pm. They don't have time to even go for a haircut outside. Remember the city is far-off. They don't have time to wash their clothes, so we provide them with a laundry service. They don't have time to go outside to shop for toothpaste and other such basic toiletries, so we have provided them a supermarket. They have no time to go into the city for recreation or sports, so we have provided them all the facilities right here. On the other hand, they are free to go to the city every weekend and they indeed do so.'

The conversation moved on to other areas, about the man, his vision and his views. Narayana Murthy was happy to express his ideas about the challenges to Infosys in the future. 'Scalability is the first one, how to keep our value system intact, how to ensure that we retain quality and productivity as the projects and clients increase. Another is to continue to attract, train, empower and retain the best and the brightest while the organization becomes larger. Also, we must continue to have acceptable margins because with growth comes a tendency to spend more without adequate returns — the margin slows down. We must become more and more multicultural to leverage high quality in our markets.

'We are No. 1 in India — the most respected, best managed company, the best employer with the best in corporate governance. Our challenge is to ensure that we are among the top five in every market we operate

— America, Europe, and Japan. How to retain the nimbleness and camaraderie, the soul of a small organization in the body of a large monolithic one — that in essence is the biggest challenge.'

Even as he spoke about the future, his mind drifted back in time...

We must accept finite disappointment,
but never lose infinite hope.

— Martin Luther King Jr —

2

# HOW IT ALL BEGAN

In those days Mysore was a sleepy little town. Although a fairly popular tourist destination in Karnataka, it did not hold the attention of the world. Much less known, back in the late 1950s and early 1960s, was that a young son of its soil was quietly maturing into a giant who would rule the globe in a unique manner.

It was the month of June in the year 1962. A serious-faced sixteen-year-old stood on the platform of Mysore railway station looking sadly after the train chugging off to Chennai (then Madras). A bunch of hands could be seen waving from one of the windows until they were lost in the smoke and distance.

They were gone. His companions through thick and thin, his boyhood friends — filled with hope, expectation, excitement and confidence — off on a journey to a new beginning. Shedding their childhood, they were to enter the larger arena of life through the gateway of a university education.

Sighing, the boy turned to leave; then changed his mind. He sat down on the iron bench on the platform, shutting his eyes to let pictures of the past flash through his mind. His mind went back to their school days, when he and his friends would study in the shade of a stone mandap near the Chamunda Hills. They would discuss the whole world, or whatever they knew of it then, arguing over issues till dusk. Of course there was serious study too — preparing for the Indian Institute of Technology (IIT) or some other competitive examination, admission to which was looked upon as the ultimate achievement. If you managed IIT, your future was made.

Preparation for such examinations in those days was quite different from what it is now. There were hardly any air-conditioned state-of-the-art coaching centres where professionals with experience had mounds of test papers and books to cater to your every need and question. The boy and his friends had no special coaching or books, just their intellect and each other's company and help, if required. And help was one thing he was always ready with. While his friends struggled with complex questions, he would solve problems of maths and physics in the blink of an eye. Shy at all other times, the subject of science would always light up his eyes.

The words of one of his friends came back to him: 'You should have made it.' Yes, he should have been on a train too, bound for IIT Kanpur, for he had sat for the entrance examination in Bangalore and ranked seventeenth. Described as the brightest boy in his class, he had given the preparation his best effort. Yet, when the relatives he was staying with asked him how he had fared, he had replied 'Okay' — his modest description of eventually emerging with flying colours and a scholarship!

How proudly he had come home and announced to his father, 'Anna, I have passed the exam. I would like to join IIT.' Putting down his newspaper, his dear father's face lit up and fell at the same time. 'I am proud of you, son. But I am sorry, I cannot afford to pay your fees, and you will get your scholarship only at the end of the year.'

Heartbroken but outwardly calm, the boy nodded quietly. He understood. His father was a school teacher in Kolar and he supported a wife and eight children on a salary of Rs 250 a month. They were actually an extended family of elven, including his grandmother. How could he demand to move ahead in life if it meant that his brothers and sisters remained uneducated? Wasn't it because of their love and support that he had come this far? They were his foundation, his rock, and he knew that they would always be there for him, through the ups and downs of life.

'Remember son,' his father had said, 'it is you and you alone who makes the change in your life, not the institution. If you are smart, you can go to any college and do something worthwhile.'

How right he was! Shaking off his reverie, the boy rose from the bench, recharged with energy. He looked around. The next train had arrived and people were jostling past him. He was hardly noticeable in a crowd, but he would stand out, some day. Now there was a new spring in his step as he strode out of the railway station.

Success is the sum of all efforts, repeated
day in and day out.

— Robert Collier —

# 3

# A HARD NUT TO CRACK

Nagavara Ramarao Narayana Murthy, better known to us today as NRNM, or the Chairman Emeritus of Infosys, was born on August 20, 1946 in a Brahmin family of Mysore. His father Nagavara Ramarao taught biology and mathematics in a high school. Nagavara had five daughters and three sons among whom Narayana Murthy was the fifth. His meagre salary was barely enough to take care of a family of eleven members. Naturally there was always shortage of money but that did not make Murthy's father hanker after money. As a teacher he was aware of the importance of education and taught his children that to lead a meaningful life education is more important than money. As a father he was a strict disciplinarian who inculcated the right values in his children. He taught his children to be honest, selfless and to care for others. Nagavara Ramarao used to be transferred every three years. So, the family had to move from town to town. These frequent transfers taught Narayana Murthy to adapt to different circumstances besides providing him the opportunity to make friends in different parts of the state and understand mofussil India. Nagavara was fond of reading English books, a habit which rubbed off on Naryana Murthy who started reading Shakespeare from an early age. Besides love for books Narayana Murthy has also inherited his father's love for Western classical music of which he  has a large collection.

Murthy's mother had studied only till the fifth standard in Kannada medium. Though not much educated herself, she knew that it was important for her children to get good education. She had to manage a large family in a meagre salary and make the most of the resources she had.  She would send her sons to get cheap timber dust to be used as fuel from a far away timber depot rather than buying it at a higher price from the local seller. From his mother Murthy learnt how to live within one's means and the values of sharing and caring. The early days of his childhood, happy but full of struggle, greatly influenced Narayana Murthy and made him the man that he is.

At school Murthy was a brilliant and popular student who always stood first in the class.  He was interested only in academics and especially loved science and mathematics. Due to his good understanding of the subjects, his class fellows and even his seniors would often approach him for clarification of their problems. Thus, seeds of a career in teaching were sown in his school days.

He had always been a hard nut to crack — literally, even as a boy! The story goes that once, while at Sharada Vilasa Boys' High School, Mysore, Murthy's class was being taught geography. The teacher was using a coconut to explain the globe to the children. Now Murthy was a real chatterbox. The teacher checked him once, 'Narayana! Be quiet, please!' But Murthy just carried on. Again, the teacher warned him. 'Didn't you hear me, Narayana?' But the boy continued talking. Losing his temper, the teacher hit him on the head with the coconut — and still Murthy's tongue kept wagging. The furious teacher hit him again with the coconut. Nobody remembers what happened to the coconut but Murthy's head remained in one piece!

Narayana Murthy took all the knocks of life in the same spirit — as a boy, young man and mature adult.

Hardly the kind to indulge in self-pity or wait for luck to favour him, the young Murthy took a practical view of his situation after completing his schooling. He knew that going to IIT Kanpur was not possible because there was not enough money in the family, so he did the next best thing. He enrolled for the Bachelor of Electrical Engineering course in the National Institute of Engineering, University of Mysore, from where he got his degree in 1967 with first position in the college. His friends during those years were Murli and Krishna, and the group was known as The Three Musketeers.

A man of many interests, Murthy was a fan of Hindi film actor-singer K.L. Saigal and English movies at the same time. One of his favourite films was 'Come September'. He loved playing around with numbers and tinkering with technology. He would dream of becoming an engineer at a hydroelectric power plant, referred to those days by Jawaharlal Nehru as 'the temples of modern India'. What he liked about them was that they were non-polluting and set in beautiful, clean surroundings. Also, being an electrical engineer and building a big generator was looked upon as very macho!

As Murthy was such a brilliant student, people advised him to continue his education and get a Master's degree. And Murthy himself knew only too well that, due to the reservation system, it would not be easy for him to get a job in Karnataka. So he postponed his career decision and enrolled for his Master's in the meantime. This time Murthy could join IIT Kanpur to do his M. Tech. in Electrical Engineering as he had received the scholarship money well in time. It was at IIT Kanpur where Murthy saw a computer for the first time. In the two years from 1967 to 1969 that Murthy was at IIT, he gained substantial knowledge about computers and their various applications.

Success is choice and opportunity.

— Harrison Ford —

# 4

# MAKING CHOICES

Narayana Murthy chose an unusual career path. Unusual, because at a time when India was facing brain-drain, thanks to the lure of dollar opportunities abroad, he refused to succumb to the temptation of no less than five lucrative overseas offers. Neither did he choose the easy way out by opting for government service at home. Perhaps his choice was the result of the varied and important influences in his life, particularly those from his early academic days.

Interestingly, that two major influences on Narayana Murthy were his namesakes — the one Narayan and the other Murthy! Murthy acknowledges, 'I've had some great teachers. I had a wonderful high school headmaster in Mysore named K.V. Narayan, when I was at Sharada Vilas High School between 1959 and 1961. Narayan was an extraordinary person and he clearly had a lasting influence on all students. Then I had professors in various stages of life who influenced me, for example, I had a professor, Dr. N. Krishna Murthy at the National Institute of Engineering, Mysore. He was a civil engineer and the first person to open our minds to what was happening outside India. I remember, he came back from the US in 1964 and opened our eyes to what was happening there. He made us realize that there are cities called New York and London and all of that.'

So, armed with a Bachelor of Engineering degree from the University of Mysore and a Master of Technology degree from IIT Kanpur, Murthy decided to take up the biggest technical challenge of the day in the emerging field of computer science. He joined the Indian Institute of Management (IIM), Ahmedabad — the best business school in India — as its very first chief systems programmer in 1969, at a meagre salary of Rs 800 a month! It was Professor Krishnayya of IIM who had convinced Murthy to take up this position, when he once visited IIT Kanpur, where Murthy was a graduate student.

Their meeting is best described in Murthy's own words: 'At breakfast on a bright Sunday morning in 1968, I had a chance encounter with a famous computer scientist from a well-known US university. He was discussing exciting new developments in the field of computer science with a large group of students and how such developments would alter our future. I was hooked. I went straight from breakfast to the library, read the four or five papers he had suggested, and left the library determined to study computer science. When I look back today at that pivotal meeting, I marvel at how one role model can alter for the better the future of a young student. This experience taught me that valuable advice can sometimes come from an unexpected source, and chance events can sometimes open new doors.'

For a man like Murthy, who loved challenges, the job at IIM was a sure carrot: IIM was to be the third business school in the world, after Harvard and Stanford, to install the modern mini-computer. What was more, there was to be a time-sharing system for the students — a golden opportunity to explore the full potential of this wonderful creation. Murthy was hooked, so much so that he forgot all boundaries of day and night. It became normal for him to work even twenty hours a day, often going home at three in the morning, to return to work seven hours later. It was the first test of Murthy's skill as an engineer. Working 24x7 under Professor Krishnayya's guidance, he helped to design and implement the first Indian BASIC computer.

Though his salary was low at IIM, this job provided Murthy the opportunity to work in the field of computers and increase his knowledge as well as experience. He describes the decision to join IIM as the best decision of his life. This was also the time when Murthy's political leanings begin to take form. He was inclined towards communism. His friends argued that he was supporting communism because his income was low and once he got a job in a big company paying good salary, he would no longer be a supporter of communism. Murthy wanted to prove them wrong. He applied for a job in Hindustan Lever Limited and was selected. But Murthy did not accept the offer. He proved his friends wrong by rejecting a job offer with good salary package  for IIM's low salary.

During his stint of three years at IIM Murthy published a research paper which earned him job offers from various companies. One of these offers came from SESA, a French company where Murthy was to work on a mega project that involved the designing and installation of a computerized cargo-handling system at Charles de Gaulle Airport in Paris. The offer had two attractions: the challenge of the job itself, and the fact that France in the early 1970s was a Left-wing country. Murthy himself had strong leanings towards the Left, having grown up with socialist sympathies, and had spent a lot of time with student activists.  It was too good a chance to miss. Murthy flew to Paris in 1972 to join SESA.

Narayana Murthy (second from left) in his younger days

Narayana Murthy at Patni Computer Systems

Narayana Murthy (extreme left) with Infosys colleagues

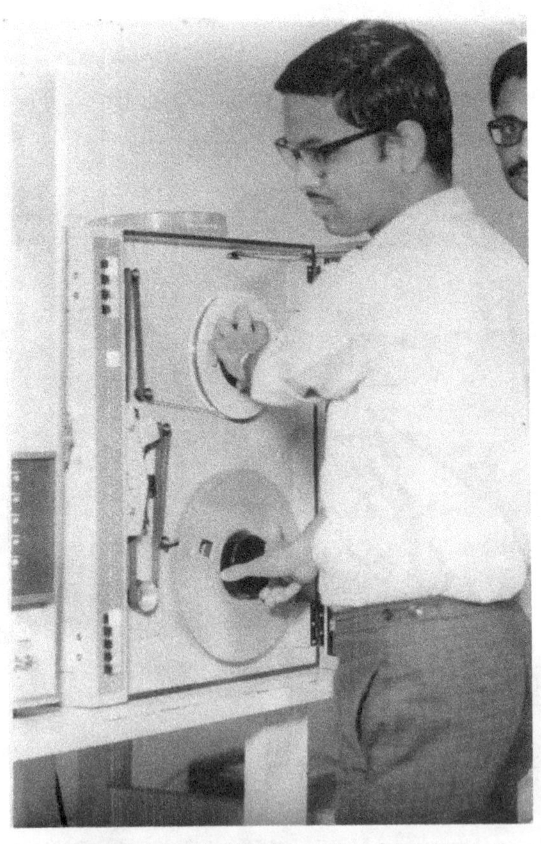

Narayana Murthy in earlier days

Narayana Murthy having breakfast in the USA

Narayana Murthy standing in front of the Infosys campus

At Nasdaq listing on 11th March, 1999

Narayana Murthy receiving Indo-French Forum Medal from former French Prime Minist
Jean-Pierre Raffarin on 13th October, 2003

Narayana Murthy receiving the Economic Times Lifetime Achievement Award from the Finance Minister on 27th October, 2007

arayana Murthy with Sudha Murthy at the Economic Times Awards ceremony to receive the Lifetime Achievement award on 27th October, 2007

Receiving an honorary doctorate from Lancaster University on 12th  December, 2007

Receiving the Padma Vibhushan award from the President of India
on 5th May, 2008

Narayana Murthy with Infoscions

Narayana Murthy receiving NDTV Lifetime Achievement Award on 1st September, 2010

Narayana Murthy (second from left in the front row) after receiving the CNBC Asia Lifetime Achievement Award on 24th November, 2011

Narayana Murthy with his daughter Akshata, son Rohan, and wife Sudha

Life is always at some turning point.

— Erwin Edman —

5

# PARIS – THE TURNING POINT

Murthy describes his stay in Paris in these words: 'My years in Paris were the most influential years of my life. I observed how in a western country even the socialists understood that wealth has first to be created before it can be distributed; that there could only be a few leaders to create wealth. And that it's the job of the government to create an environment where it's possible for people to create wealth. I realized that all this talk of socialism as practised in India was not meaningful. Our country treated communism as an 'ism' that was completely dissociated from the reality of the context. You cannot distribute poverty.' In Paris Murthy's eyes were opened to the prosperity enjoyed by capitalist Europe, which set him questioning his previous beliefs. 'I realized that even the worst communists believe that you have to work hard, there's a role for the private sector, and that the only solution to create wealth is to encourage more and more people to create wealth rather than redistribute poverty.'

However, for this realization to sink in took time and something more. At SESA, Murthy worked with the same zeal and energy as he had at IIM. Taking the project at Charles de Gaulle airport to its successful completion in 1974, he was ready for change once again. Then still a socialist at heart, he gave away all his savings to charity and, with nothing more than a backpack, made his way via land to India, with the intention of visiting all the communist countries on the way. Those were, for him, recalls Murthy, '… the halcyon days of socialism, the glory days of the Soviet Union. For those of us from developing countries, the fact that America refused to build a steel plant in India while the Soviet Union did, made us glorify socialism. And the primary tenet of socialism was that wealth should be distributed among all members of society.'

Travel became an important part of Murthy's life and entailed certain experiences that left an impact on him. In his own words, 'An event that left an indelible mark on me occurred in 1974. The location: Nis, a border town between former Yugoslavia (now Serbia) and Bulgaria. I was hitchhiking from Paris back to Mysore. By the time a kind driver dropped me at Nis railway station at 9 pm on a Saturday, the restaurants were closed. So was the bank the next morning, being a Sunday, and I could not eat because I had no local money. I slept on the railway platform until the Sofia Express pulled in. The only passengers in my compartment were a girl and a boy. I struck a conversation in French with the young girl. She talked about the travails of living in an iron curtain country, until we were roughly interrupted by some policemen who, I later gathered, were summoned by the young man who thought we were criticizing the communist government of Bulgaria. The girl was led away and my backpack and sleeping bag were confiscated. I was dragged along the platform into a small 8x8 foot room with a cold stone floor and a hole in one corner by way of toilet facilities. I was held in that bitterly cold room without food or water for over 72 hours.

I had lost all hope of ever seeing the outside world again, when the door opened. I was again dragged out unceremoniously, locked up in the guard's compartment on a departing freight train and told that I would be released 20 hours later upon reaching Istanbul. The guard's final words still ring in my ears: "You are from a friendly country called India and that is why we are letting you go!"

The journey to Istanbul was lonely, and I was starving. This long, cold journey forced me to deeply rethink my convictions about communism. Early on a dark Thursday morning, after being hungry for 108 hours, I was purged of any last vestiges or affinity for the Left. I concluded that entrepreneurship, resulting in large-scale job creation, was the only viable mechanism for eradicating poverty in societies.

Deep in my heart, I always thank the Bulgarian guards for transforming me from a confused Leftist into a determined, compassionate capitalist!'

The wheel had been set in motion. It would be no exaggeration to say that this sequence of events eventually led to the founding of Infosys six years later in 1981.

A good marriage is one which allows for change
and growth in the individuals.

— Pearl S Buck —

6

# AN 'UNSUITABLE' BOY

With body and mind reaching out to new horizons, how could the heart and soul be left behind? Murthy's soulmate-to-be, Sudha, was then working with Telco in Pune.

Born on 19 August, 1950, Sudha Kulkarni belongs to a middle class family in Karnataka. Her father, H.R. Kulkarni was a doctor in a government hospital. When Sudha joined BVR Engineering College in Hubli she became the first girl of her town to join an engineering college.

During the five years of her engineering course Sudha faced many problems in college. The boys were biased against her and often ragged her. She did not take leave even for a day as the boys would not share their notes of the previous days' classes with her. As there had been no girl in the college before Sudha, it did not have a ladies toilet; Sudha often had to wait long agonising hours till she reached home. Instead of disheartening her, these difficulties motivated her to outperform her classmates which she did; she achieved the highest score in all the ten semesters. This was not the only instance when she proved herself the best among her peers. In 1974, she came first in her M.Tech. class at Indian Institute of Science (IISc) in Bangalore.

Sudha had topped every exam she ever sat for; naturally, she aspired for the best career-wise too. One day she saw a recruitment advertisement of Telco which stated that 'Ladies need not apply.' Telco, a Tata company, engaged in the manufacture of heavy vehicles, was looking to recruit young engineers. Seething against this unfairness, Sudha wasted no time in penning a letter to JRD Tata, the then chairman of the Tata group of companies, suggesting that if Telco did not hire her, the loss would be theirs, not hers! JRD called her for an interview and was so impressed with her that he immediately changed the company policy and hired this spirited young lady! Sudha created history by being the first woman to be recruited as an engineer in Telco, where she worked for the next eight years.

Meanwhile, the young Narayana Murthy, still recovering from the recent Bulgarian experience, had returned to India, only to find that the situation in his home country was rather bleak. Prime Minister Indira Gandhi had declared Emergency and the environment, especially for business, was unwelcoming and hostile. Despite that Murthy was determined to be an entrepreneur and a wealth-creator. In 1975 with one of his college professors he started System Research Institute (SRI) in Pune with the objective of using computer software applications to improve the efficiency of cargo movement and handling at airports. This software could also be used for improving road facilities and electricity and water management. But SRI could find no takers for its applications.

Murthy met Sudha in Pune where she was working for Telco. Her colleague, Prasanna who later became Wipro chief, would often lend her books as she was fond of reading. She noticed that many of the books had the name Murthy written on them. On her asking Prasanna told her about Murthy and his interest in reading. Without seeing Murthy, Sudha had formed an image of Murthy in her mind which proved quite to the contrary when she actually met him. Shortly after, Murthy invited her to dinner. Sudha was surprised, because he seemed rather shy and introverted. She thought he was moving too fast, and so she refused.

But, where there is a will there is a way and Murthy did not give up till she agreed to meet him for dinner at the Green Fields Hotel. Gradually they discovered they had a lot in common, and soon their friendship began to grow. Despite Murthy's ordinary appearance Sudha began to like him. She was attracted by Murthy's expertise in his field, his ideas, vision, and confidence. What Murthy loved about Sudha were her positive outlook and her empathy for the poor. They spoke at length about Murthy's experiences abroad and the books they read. Sudha's friends teased her about Murthy's affection for her but she denied it until the day he finally popped the question. Sudha's version of his proposal is, 'I am 5' 4" tall. I come from a lower middle class family. I can never become rich in my life and I can never give you any riches. You are beautiful, bright, and intelligent and you can get anyone you want. But will you marry me?'

Hardly a rosy picture for a wife-to-be! But Sudha's heart was equally involved, so she asked for time to think. Then, of course, she had to put the matter to her parents — not an easy task! The response was predictable. Sudha's father wanted to know: what Murthy did for a living, how much he earned, and what his future plans were — in that order. And promptly rejected him because Murthy was a partner in a new venture with the order book virtually blank and he earned less than Sudha. How on earth could Sudha expect to be happy with such a man? In contrast, her mother's view was positive: after all, the boy hailed from the same state, Karnataka, seemed intelligent and came from a good family — basic ingredients for a happy marriage.

After much debate, Sudha's parents agreed to meet Murthy on a particular day at 10 am. But Murthy did not turn up at the appointed hour! 'A man who cannot keep his appointment is not fit to take care of my daughter,' announced Sudha's father. Still, they waited and at 12 noon the son-in-law to be arrived — in a bright red shirt. He apologized, 'I'm sorry. I went to work in Bombay and got stuck in a traffic jam. Finally I hired a taxi, although it is beyond my budget.'

'Hmph,' muttered the would-be father-in-law, expressing his sentiments very clearly. Then he asked Murthy about his plans in life. When Murthy replied that he wanted to join the Communist Party and also open an orphanage, Sudha's father said 'Nothing doing!' Thus ended their first meeting.

By now, however, Sudha had realized that she had found the man she wanted to spend her life with. She told her father that she would not marry Murthy without his blessings. In the same breath she said that she would not marry anybody except Murthy! Knowing his daughter well, Sudha's father said he would agree if Murthy took on a steady job, but Murthy stated that he would not do so just because someone said he should! Thus Sudha was caught between the obstinacy of the two most important men in her life.

Things remained like this for the next two years. During this time Sudha and Murthy continued to meet, visiting nearly every restaurant and cinema hall in Pune. They used to visit a Chinese restaurant where they could eat for only Rs. 9. They often went Dutch but most of the time Sudha paid the bills as she was the one with the steady job. Murthy said he would repay her later and she even kept an account of what he owed her, tearing it up only after they were married!

After two years of struggle at SRI, Murthy left his first entrepreneurial venture and moved to Mumbai to join Patni Computers Systems (PCS) as a general manager in August 1977. But he wanted to marry Sudha before that. Fairly satisfied that Murthy was now on a stable track, Sudha's father agreed. In Sudha's words, they 'were married in Murthy's house in Bangalore on February 10, 1978, with only our two families present. I got my first silk sari. The wedding expenses came to only Rs. 800, with Murthy and I pooling in Rs. 400 each'. They were keeping up the Dutch tradition!

After the wedding they went to the US where Murthy had to undergo training. An enthusiastic traveller, Sudha accompanied him and toured America with a backpack and had a couple of interesting experiences. Recalling that time, she says the New York police once took her into custody because they thought she was an Italian dealing in drugs in Harlem! And another time she ended up spending a night with an old couple at the bottom of the Grand Canyon while a frantic Murthy, who was unable to contact her, had visions of her being killed or kidnapped!

Coming together is a beginning,
staying together is progress,
and working together is success.

— Henry Ford —

# 7

# NEW BEGINNINGS

On return from the USA, Murthy and Sudha set up their first home together in Mumbai in Bandra. Sudha had to leave her job at Telco in Pune, but Telco was loath to let a competent person like her go, so they offered her a job in their office in the Fort area in Mumbai.

At Patni, Murthy was in charge of the software department. And it was here that he met one of his future Infosys partners, Nandan Nilekani. Patni was fast expanding and needed people for it. Nandan Nilekani, an engineer from IIT Mumbai, applied to Patni for a job and was taken on. Murthy took an instant liking to this young man who shared Murthy's passion for work and new ideas. Soon they became good friends and so did their wives Sudha and Rohini. The software industry at the  time in India, was in its infancy; but people like Murthy and Nilekani could envision the exciting possibilities that it offered and they hungered to explore the unchartered territories which lay ahead. Work at Patni did offer them the opportunity to work in the sunrise software industry but not at the pace which Murthy had in mind. Or was it the entrepreneurial bug which had bitten Murthy again!

Often, Murthy would discuss with Nilekani what he saw as the potential of software applications and what was needed to realize this potential. Nilekani was equally upbeat about the industry  potential and just like Murthy was beginning to be a little stifled at what he perceived as the slow approach at Patni. Joining in these discussions were a few other like-minded young men at Patni who were fired up to achieve something path-breaking, something new. This group had by now seven people including Murthy and they were all ready to quit the safe haven of Patni and enter headlong into the promising new world of computer applications.

All great things have small beginnings.

— Peter Senge —

# 8

# THE
# MAGNIFICENT SEVEN

June 1981. Grabbing a quick lunch in the canteen of Patni Computer Systems, sat the 'magnificent seven'. At least that is how they had begun to refer to themselves, after the 'big bright idea' had taken hold of their minds. Murthy and his six friends wanted to start a software company which would develop software for foreign clients and offer offshore computer services. In those days a simple enough task like importing computers into the country was a Herculean task and also the seven friends did not have the capital to fund their venture. But still they were confident that they could pull it off as each of them was an expert in his area of work and had the required experience.

'The time has come. Let's do it, guys,' announced Murthy.

'Are you sure?' asked Shibu.

'Perhaps we should wait till things stabilize a little,' suggested Nandan, toying with his cutlery.

Holding up his glass and peering through it as if it were a crystal bowl, Kris stated philosophically, 'Now is as good a time as any. Who knows what the future will hold?'

'You haven't said anything yet, Dinesh,' remarked Murthy.

'See, I believe we ought to start on a sure footing, sufficient funds and all.'

'I disagree,' responded Ashok. 'We're young, we can take the strain now, and I guess so can our wives! A few years down the line, the passion just might wane.'

'The passion will never wane, that's for sure,' stated Murthy, pushing his chair back. 'Time to get back to work. Let's sleep on it and take a decision tomorrow.'

As they lay in bed that night, the stars visible in the clear, dark sky from their window, Sudha said, 'Out with it, Murthy. What's on your mind?'

'Mind? Nothing…I mean, how did you know?'

'I am your wife, remember? And anyway, you never were a good pretender.'

Murthy had actually been waiting for an opportunity

to broach the subject. Glad to get it off his chest at last, he eagerly told her of his discussions with their friends earlier in the day. Despite the inhibitions of some of their friends, Murthy was convinced that it was now or never. He was prepared to take the plunge, and didn't chance favour the prepared mind?

'You know my firm belief in Gandhiji's advice, Sudha — You must be the change you wish to see in the world — and I want to make that change now.'

'You mean you want to quit your job at Patni?' asked Sudha, more as a statement of fact than a question.

'We would have to — all seven of us. There's no other way. You can't do things by halves; we must give it all we have,' defended Murthy.

'Hmm, and we don't have much! Between the two of us, at least…If you gave up your job, mine would be the only income. Would we be able to sustain ourselves on it? More important, do we have enough for your venture to take off?'

'We do require a sum to begin with. Just so we can get a computer or two. Office is no problem, we'll work from home until…'

'How much?' asked Sudha.

'What?'

'How much do you need to start off?'

'About ten thousand rupees should be enough.'

Sudha did not have the required money but suddenly she recalled something. When Sudha was getting married to Narayana Murthy her mother had advised her to save some money every month for any contingency. At that time Sudha did not think that there would be any such situation ever but nevertheless she followed her mother's advice. She started putting aside the money which was left over after meeting the monthly household expenses. She had almost forgotten about that money. When she counted her savings, Sudha found that she had just the much needed money to finance her husband's venture.

Though Sudha was not sure whether Murthy should take the risk of quitting his job to start business, she decided to support his decision and gave him Rs. 10,000. But she laid down a condition for Murthy.

'I'll grant you a three-year sabbatical to make this work. After that, if it doesn't, back to square one. You'll have to find a job.'

'Done,' said Murthy. 'Good night!' And fell asleep the minute his head touched the pillow.

Smiling mischievously, Sudha switched off the light and slid under the covers.

Murthy and his friends resigned from their jobs at Patni by the end of 1980 but finished all their tasks before leaving. The en masse resignations of Murthy and his group sparked many rumours and accusations. Two decades later in an interview in 2002, Patni's founder, Narendra Patni, accused that Murthy and his friends had poached Patni's clients. But Murthy emphatically denied the allegations saying none of Patni's clients had shifted to Infosys.

On July 2, 1981, Murthy and his six colleagues — Nandan Nilekani, S. Kris Gopalakrishnan, S.D. Shibulal, N.S. Raghavan, K. Dinesh and Ashok Arora came together in a 120 sq.ft. apartment in Pune  to give a name to their dream — Infosys. Although they did not have what is usually considered the necessary resources to start an organization, they had each other, the support of their wives, determination and a positive attitude. The company was incorporated as Infosys Consultants Pvt. Ltd., with its registered office at Raghavan's house in Matunga, Mumbai. Eleven years later, in 1992, the name was changed to 'Infosys Technologies Ltd.'

Like little drops of water that make the mighty ocean, the magnificent seven marched ahead to make their mark in the corporate world. From their early humble beginnings, they became the foundation of an organization that would command the respect, admiration and envy of everyone in the Information Technology (IT) industry, in India and the world over.

Quality is never an accident; it is always the
result of intelligent effort.

— John Ruskin —

# 9

# 'POWERED BY INTELLECT, DRIVEN BY VALUES'

This has been Narayana Murthy's motto throughout life — in the personal as well as professional sphere — and he has followed it so diligently as to make it an example to emulate. His vision was clear, but the path un-trodden; it was their unwavering belief in their mission that held the seven friends and colleagues in good stead, enabling them to surge ahead, crossing every pothole and weathering every storm.

Starting a new business in those days was very difficult. There were no angel investors to fund business start-ups. What Murthy and his friends had collected was just a meagre sum and they actually needed a large amount to set up a world class company which could compete with the best in the industry and the world. Banks refused to give any loan as the software industry was at a nascent stage in India and nobody was sure about its prospects.  Despite all these problems the seven were determined to pursue their dreams.

In the founding of Infosys, with the ultimate goal of creating wealth for all its stakeholders, Murthy was guided by three major principles which are adhered to even today. One, the company is primarily transaction based and not personality driven. Therefore, its management focuses on what is best for the company, regardless of individual personality issues. Two, as is clearly reflected in its management compensation and planning, Infosys focuses on long-term goals and objectives. Three, there is no blurring of the boundary between corporate and personal resources. All employees are urged to be cost conscious.

Many years later, Murthy still remembers how as a school boy he was first made aware of that boundary. He relates the story of a chemistry teacher who was conducting an experiment in the science laboratory of the school. One of the ingredients required for the experiment was salt. The teacher began measuring out the salt carefully, a little too carefully according to the students who went into a giggling fit. It was only common salt after all. Where was the need to be so careful? That's when the teacher looked up and admonished them, saying that it wasn't his salt or their salt but salt bought from school funds which made it obligatory for them to ensure nothing was wasted.

As Murthy puts it, 'Values was something Infosys never compromised upon, no matter what the hardships. In those days it would take anywhere between fifteen to twenty-four months to get a computer. We started in 1981 but our first computer was installed only in February 1984. Getting a loan was very difficult. We had worked out a time-sharing deal with Mico on the basis of which ANZ Grindlays Bank did a project report. But the bank refused to give us the loan. Several other banks also turned us down. It was just by chance on a flight that I happened to be sitting next to K.S.N. Murthy of the Karnataka State Industrial Investment and Development Corporation, and we got our break. They redid the entire project report working fourteen hours a day for a week and got it sanctioned in fifteen days.'

'Right from day one our idea was to add value from India. To do that we needed at the very least — computers and telephone lines. It took us a year to get a phone in Bangalore. There was a rule then that higher priority was to be given to retired government servants rather than businesses. We already had a contract for $3,50,000; in addition we would get an IBM-compatible machine on loan from our customer. All that they insisted was that we have a telephone so that they could contact us. The customer said: "Look I understand that you are a group of competent people, but if you want to do it from India you must convince us that you can establish a line of communication." So, much against our desire, we had to ship the team out.'

'One has to go through all these experiences because it makes you understand your own frailties and also helps you develop respect for God. I've been extraordinarily lucky in life. I've received much more from society than I've given. I have many friends who are much smarter, much more accomplished, but somehow life has dealt me so many good cards that I can't ascribe it to anything other than God's grace.'

Murthy was fortunate that Sudha had agreed to pay his salary for the determined period of three years, because for Infosys, the initial ten years were a struggle, the company barely managing to pay the employees' salaries. Still, the seven dreamers-founders were young, their will strong and spirit undying. Moreover, they believed in a transparent set-up, where each could freely voice his opinion and all agree to disagree, as long as their arguments and brainstorming led them forward, closer to their goal and they were not disagreeable! In fact, transparency remains a feature of the organization even today.

In 1981, when Infosys was started, Murthy and Sudha lived in Mumbai where Sudha was working for Telco. Murthy had to travel regularly to Pune where Infosys was situated. This arrangement was time-consuming, and put a lot of financial and physical strain on Murthy. As it made more sense to live in Pune, Murthy bought a house in Pune. Sudha sold some of her jewellery to arrange part of the money needed to buy the house. It was a two-room apartment shared by the two families of Murthy and Nandan Nilekani besides being used as the office of Infosys. Sudha and Nandan Nilekani's wife Rohini used to do the household chores besides helping with the office work such as answering telephone calls, managing correspondence, making tea for the staff as Infosys did not have the money to employ staff for such work. In an interview to Financial Express Sudha says, 'It was really hectic. I was the receptionist-cum-clerk-cum- programmer, and had to look after organizing everything. But it was beautiful working towards that dream.' In Pune Sudha was working for Walchand Computers at that time whose office was four kilometres away from Sudha's place but she walked to it instead of using a conveyance as she wanted to save money to repay the loan they had taken for the home. As it was the first home which Murthys bought, Sudha was emotionally attached to it. Later in 1983 when Infosys was shifted to Banglore and the house was sold, Sudha wept for many days.

Murthy had to make tough decisions and make sacrifices for the sake of Infosys. He was not with his children during their growing up years. When his son Rohan was born, he had to leave for US for work; he could see his son only after a year. Murthy acknowledges that his wife had to raise the children single-handedly, 'She understood that a company like Infosys demands passion, commitment and all of your time.'

There were reasons (apart from their own financial and infrastructural constraints) for the difficulties that Infosys faced in the initial period of its growth. Prior to 1991, the economic scenario in India was hardly favourable to a rapid rise of the information technology industry. There was an institutional void in product markets and a dearth of quality hardware. The capital markets were insufficient, as a result of which new entrepreneurs had very limited availability of finance. Besides, there were limitations of the labour markets, the visa restrictions preventing mobility of talent across borders. The bureaucratic red tape also made things difficult for Infosys. It took two years for Murthy to get official permission to import a computer. Infosys could get a telephone connection only after trying for a year. Till then, they made business calls from a public phone booth. It would take ten days to get foreign exchange for travelling abroad.

Despite these hurdles, the founders of Infosys knew where to place their limited bucks. They knew that there was hardly any market for software services in India. Hence, from the very start, the company concentrated on overseas business which gave it a global perspective that many other Indian companies lacked. It was not easy to get overseas clients as Infosys was a new service provider in the market and the clients needed to be convinced that Infosys could offer good quality of work. Infosys had to compete with the domestic US companies and the companies from other countries. While Murthy remained in India, generating business and managing the corporate office and administrative issues, the other founders travelled to the US, often staying for months at a time to execute on-site programming for corporate clients. To keep costs low and within budget, they resorted to sharing cheap apartments, cooking their own food, walking or taking a bus and any other way that could help them save their scarce finances. From time to time Murthy and his friends would get job offers from foreign companies but they chose to remain with Infosys.

Back home, Murthy set an example by following the principle of simple living and high thinking. It is said that he went to meet his first client on a bicycle. The remarkable part is that this simplicity is not an appearance but an essential part of the man himself. Murthys did not have TV at home till their son was 12 years old. Till date he does not go in for expensive designer suits or over-the-top travel — he flies economy class! And he continues to live with wife Sudha in their modest three-bedroom flat on Hosur Road, Bangalore. Naturally, these values filtered top-down and soon became an integral part of the company.

To make Infosys a world class company and to gain a foothold in the foreign markets Murthy made some rules for the company to follow. His first rule was that the software written by them should completely fulfil the requirement of the clients. The quality of their services should be the best. Another point on which Murthy put emphasis was that the software developed by them should not be area-specific or country-specific but should be global as they could have clients from anywhere in the world. Infosys also had the advantage of lower costs as India was cheaper than other countries.

Infosys hired its first employees in 1982. They were three young engineers from IIT Chennai. Murthy recalls, 'We had very little to offer our first employees and so attracting talent was extremely difficult. All I could promise them was tremendous opportunities to grow and learn, and a work environment that would never be lacking challenge!'

He has not forgotten their reaction on joining work. 'They were really surprised when they showed up the first day for work and discovered that the office, which all three would have to share with me, was a converted bedroom in my little apartment.' Nevertheless, the passion to make a mark proved infectious and the youngsters stayed on. Infosys trained each of its early employees at its offices in India and then dispatched them to work at client sites in the US.

Over time there was an increase in the company's revenues which enabled it to invest in resources for training and product development. The 1980s was a time when the Indian economy was closed to outside investment and the policy context was heavily bureaucratic. India did not manufacture any computers indigenously then, and even a relatively simple task like applying for an import licence required a company to prove that it was generating significant revenues in foreign exchange. As a matter of course, these licences took many months to approve. Some companies actually maintained a staff to negotiate with government offices to approve their licences.

Although all of its revenues came from foreign markets, Infosys had neither the capacity to incur the cost of purchasing and maintaining its own computer in India nor the space to keep it. But would Murthy and his team give up on account of such minor hurdles?

In characteristic style, the founders found an ingenious solution with scarce resources. Infosys purchased the computer and had it installed on the premises of a major customer in India. To top it all, it imparted technical knowledge in exchange for computer time; and at the same time, it used the computer to train new employees and develop products. Thus it killed two birds with one stone — it realized revenues and gained a valuable tool for training while addressing the costs of maintenance and storage.

A chain of events had been set in motion by now. From a capital-starved operation, Infosys began offering on-site services to foreign customers, and then turned into a provider of turnkey software development and maintenance. 'On-site services was a step in confidence building with our customers. Most of them did not know of our capability and we had to make them feel comfortable with our model before moving our software development offshore to India. We also focused on acquiring domain knowledge in key vertical segments such as retail, distribution, finance, and telecommuni-cation,' explains Murthy.

One of the takers for the company's low-cost, high quality customized software solutions was sports shoemaker Reebok International Ltd. Murthy observed that his company's client base was growing and he decided to set up software factories in India to take advantage of lower costs and economies of scale while implementing processes and systems that would allow it to gain a strategic advantage for future customers.

In 1983, Infosys shifted its headquarters to Bangalore. It was the first software company to set up office in Bangalore. There were various reasons behind this decision. Compared with Pune and Mumbai, Bangalore was a cheaper city besides having better infrastructure and connectivity which enabled Infosys to cut operating costs and increase its profit. Moving to Bangalore had another advantage for Infosys. The southern India had good engineering colleges from where Infosys could recruit fresh talent. The most important and the immediate reason was that Infosys had got work from a German mechanical engineering company MICO. The condition was that the work had to be done in Bangalore. Narayana Murthy and N S Raghavan went to MICO's office to sign the agreement on a friend's scooter which surprised MICO's director who asked them to hire a taxi next time.

At that time Sudha wanted to formally join Infosys but Murthy was against the move. There were two reasons for his decision. First, if both of them worked for Infosys, their children would be neglected which Murthy did not want. Secondly, he did not want to give the impression that Sudha was in Infosys simply because she was his wife, though Sudha was well qualified to join Infosys and the directors of the company welcomed her. Murthy told Sudha that he was willing to quit Infosys if she wanted to join it as only one of them could work for it. Sudha decided against joining Infosys. She made this sacrifice for the sake of Murthy as she believed 'His dreams are far superior to my dreams.'

Four years later, Infosys got its first foreign client,

Data Basics Corporation from the US. In the same year, it also opened its first international office in the US, in Fremont, California, which is now its US headquarters. In 1989, Ashok Arora left Infosys to join a US-based software company.  There were many balls to be kept in the air at the same time and some were bound to fall.

A time came, in 1989, when Infosys was on the brink of bankruptcy. Murthy recalls, 'On a chilly Saturday morning in winter 1990, five of the seven founders of Infosys met in our small office in Bangalore. The decision at hand was the possible sale of Infosys for the enticing sum of $1 million. After nine years of toil in the then business-unfriendly India, we were quite happy at the prospect of seeing some money. I let my younger colleagues talk about their future plans. Discussions about the travails of our journey thus far and our future challenges went on for about four hours. I had not yet spoken a word. Finally, it was my turn. I spoke about our journey from a small Mumbai apartment in 1981 that had been beset with many challenges but also of how I believed we were at the darkest hour before dawn. I then took an audacious step. If they were all bent upon selling the company, I said, I would buy out all my colleagues though I did not have a cent in my pocket. There was a stunned silence in the room. My colleagues wondered aloud about my foolhardiness. But I remained silent. However, after an hour of my arguments, my colleagues changed their minds. I urged them that if we wanted to create a great company, we should be optimistic and confident. In minutes, they all said that we're with you. From now onwards we will never discuss the issue of closing down, getting tired or giving up. This marathon will be restarted.'

With renewed vigour and determination, they doubled their efforts to achieve their goals. Fortunately, it was not long before a foreign exchange crisis forced India to 'open up' or liberalize. Most of the earlier constraints were removed with the relaxation of barriers to the flow of people, capital and ideas. Now Infosys software engineers could be relocated to their customer sites without much ado, and the Infosys management did not have to spend indefinite hours circumventing regulations in New Delhi. There was better access to foreign know-how regarding the IT industry as also to equity capital which was available locally through listings.

With 1991 began the years of triumph, without a backward glance. Software headhunting corporations like GE, Reebok and Nortel began to focus their attention on India. In 1992 Infosys registered itself as a public limited company in India and the feathers in its cap began to increase more rapidly than you could count them.

If you're walking down the right path and
you're willing to keep walking, eventually
you'll make progress.

— Barack Obama —

# 10

# THE GLOBAL PLAYFIELD

The IT boom had already begun in most of the Western world, and was about to make its force felt in India. Infosys was only one of the players in the field, and still a small one. Was it sheer intuition that had led Narayana Murthy to plunge into this industry? Was it a sharp, futuristic vision or simply a shot in the dark? Perhaps he had keenly observed the progress of the global information technology industry and come to recognize the signs of the success that was to be.

The IT industry has many facets. It offers hardware, software, and related services. The birth of this industry can be traced back to 1946, the year when the Moore

School of Engineering at the University of Pennsylvania in Philadelphia created the ENIAC — the first electronic computer. Today we take the near-invisible microchips for granted but the first computers were extremely bulky. Wiring and parts included, they often filled up entire rooms!

It was a series of inventions that boosted the sales of the IT industry to over $55 million by the year 1980. The world got an audio blessing in the transistor in 1948, the highly useful integrated circuit in 1958, and that wonderful creation, the microprocessor, in the early 1970s. The final spurt was provided by the introduction of the Personal Computer in the late 1970s, resulting in the rapid speeding up of industry growth. At the time, IBM — the technology giant and monopoly — was known to people within the industry as the 'Big Blue'. There soon emerged many offshoots like Microsoft, Apple Computer, Sun Microsystems, and Oracle Corporation. Within the next twenty-odd years, the global annual revenues of the IT industry had crossed $360 billion, making it the world's largest single industry.

Keeping a close eye on these developments, Murthy slowly but steadily steered his organization up the corporate ladder. He knew the horizon was far but reachable. A perfectionist to the core, he preferred to concentrate on building a team that would stand the test of time rather than make quick bucks while the going was good or by taking shortcuts. Once, when asked what distinguished Infosys from many other companies, this is what its founder said: 'We have a very strong value system. In fact, when I address new employees, the main thing I talk to them about is the value system. I tell them that even in the fiercest competitive situation they must never talk ill of customers. For heaven's sake don't short-change anybody. Never ever violate any law of the land. It is better to lose a billion dollars than a good night's sleep.'

To begin with, IT markets were mainly concentrated in the developed countries. In 1990, 80% of all IT spending was by the top six countries. While the US accounted for almost 35% of the market, Japan made up another 19%, followed by Germany, which had a share of 8%. The acceleration of growth was remarkable: the US market was progressing at about 7% per year and markets in other countries were not far behind, with Japan and Germany experiencing a growth of 13% and 10% respectively. The top six countries comprised 75% of all IT spending by 1995.

At the same time, other countries in Europe began to increase their expenditure on items related to IT. For instance, in 1990, hardware accounted for about 50% of IT revenues worldwide. However, this share began to decline because of advancements in the development of microprocessors. On a global basis, hardware shipments shot up by 8%, from $ 437.5 billion in 1996 to an estimated $ 475.5 billion in 1997. Top of the global list of computer market areas was the North American market, comprising the US, Canada, and Mexico, accounting for 44% of the total in 1997. The European market, which includes the Western European countries, was the second largest, representing 35.6% of worldwide shipments, while Asia made up about 17% of the total worldwide computer shipments. By 1998, the average price of a PC had slid to about $1,000. In fact, there was now a flourishing 'sub-1000' market, which had an increasing number of machines for under $ 600. By this time, hardware accounted for about 35% of all IT spending and customers were spending more to obtain quality software and services.

The 1990s and after saw the emergence of software and services as the most dynamic segment of the IT industry, with a Compound Annual Growth Rate (CAGR) of 15% as against 6% for hardware. The former also proved to be the most profitable, with an average return on sales of over 10% for packaged software and 7% for professional services. Conversely, hardware producers faced a hard time, with a margin close to zero.

The packaged software category of the IT industry represented software such as operating systems, word processors, spreadsheets, databases, presentation graphics, financial/tax software, entertainment programs, home education, and desktop publishing programs. These were easily available in the market for a price. Leaders in this segment were manufacturers of large-scale proprietary systems, like IBM, which was a rare case of a company being a leader in both hardware and software.

Most firms, however, were not as fortunate. Many did not possess sufficient resources to create and maintain the numerous and varied skills required to design, install, and integrate increasingly diverse and sophisticated hardware and software applications. Programmers and analysts preferred to work for computer services companies, because here they could avail of better on-going education programmes that enabled them to remain on the leading edge of technology.

Some developing countries and offshore locations allowed companies that outsourced to take advantage of significant cost savings. For instance, India, China, Philippines, and Mexico had talented pools of programmers who worked for one-fourth the cost of similar programmers in the US and Japan.

Significant improvements in infrastructure around this time also helped to give a boost to the demand for IT services. There was major improvement in the technological capabilities of the telecom industry. More bandwidths were now available for data transmission, making transmission of software over communication lines reliable. In tandem with this significant increase in demand for IT services, the supply of qualified IT professionals had decreased in most developed countries, particularly in the US, Western Europe, and Japan. According to the US Department of Education, the number of bachelor degrees awarded in computer science annually at US universities came down from 41,889 in 1986 to 24,404 in 1995. This resulted in a growing shortage of IT professionals in the market. According to the Information Technology Association of America, US companies having more than 100 employees had as many as 346,000 unfilled positions for IT professionals in January 1998. To make matters worse, the US Department of Commerce estimated that between 1994 and 2005, the requirement for US companies would be more than one million IT professionals, in order to fill newly created positions and replace retiring workers. A solution to the problem was found by outsourcing software development and maintenance projects to offshore IT service providers. Through this method, companies were able to enjoy the services of skilled IT professionals, often in lower-cost environments, with a large population of English-speaking technical talent. One such environment was India.

The secret of success in life is for a man to be
ready for his opportunity when it comes.

— Benjamin Disraeli —

# 11

# THE ERA OF LIBERALIZATION

'Chance favours the prepared mind. Just as we got determined to run the marathon with much greater gusto, liberalization happened. If there is one company that symbolizes all the good that came out of liberalization, it is Infosys,' says Murthy.

The times were changing. The world had shrunk, at least in terms of ideas and interaction, to one global village. Naturally, what was happening in one part of the hemisphere could not fail to have an impact on the other.

Thus far, India had kept a tight rein of control on its economy and entry of outsiders. Despite its good intentions, this policy was no longer feasible nor possible, in its own interest. In 1991, the Government of India announced a number of measures to address the economic and financial difficulties the country had been facing. These included policies that were aimed at stimulating investment in infrastructure industries. In addition, there were favourable incentives designed to nurture the growing Indian software industry.

Ironically, this was also a time of political instability in the country. The government changed as often as five times between 1991 and 1998; the remarkable thing to note was that each government during this period committed itself to supporting the software sector. This was exemplified in the establishment of a National Task Force on Information Technology by the Indian government in May 1998. This Task Force had a mandate to make recommendations for detailing policies to increase India's IT exports. Software firms heaved a sigh of relief, thanks to an additional variety of incentives, such as exemption from import duties on hardware; a tax deduction for income derived from software exports, and tax holidays and infrastructure support for companies operating in Software Technology Parks. These policies had helped the Indian software industry enjoy a compound annual growth rate of almost 52% from 1992 to 1998. In an interview with Business Week magazine in June 1998, Murthy stated that a lot of these factors were responsible for Infosys' meteoric rise in revenues. 'We were very, very, lucky,' he says. 'But then chance favours the prepared mind and we were preparing ourselves for this day for a long time, almost eleven years, and when it happened, we seized it with both hands.'

India's visibility in the global IT industry had certainly begun to increase. According to a survey of US software companies conducted by the World Bank in 1997, India was the leading offshore destination for companies seeking to outsource software development or IT projects. An estimate by the National Association of Software and Service Companies (NASSCOM) in India stated that India's export revenue from software, including software services, was close to Rs 64 billion in 1997-1998 and was likely to touch Rs 365 billion by 2001. Of the Indian software export market, the US accounted for close to 58% of business, and Europe accounted for 21%.

Riding the high tide, the Indian software industry had shifted its focus to a greater concentration on application software development which was one of the fastest growing sectors of the software industry. Business Today, a leading Indian business magazine, conducted a survey in 1998, the result of which showed that India's software export market had grown by over 50% between 1997-98 and 1998-99.

While there is no debating the fact that economic liberalization in India has been a key factor in making India a premier source for software services, two other factors were also important. One, the expertise of a large, highly skilled labour pool that is available for a relatively low cost. Boasting of over four million engineers, India ranks second only to the US as the country with the largest population of English-speaking technical personnel.

According to NASSCOM, the number of software professionals employed by Indian companies grew from approximately 56,000 in 1990 to just over 200,000 in 1998. In addition, India has over 1, 800 engineering colleges which annually train an estimated 68,000 graduates in IT. According to Software Producti-vity Research, a research organization concentrating on the software industry, the average annual wage for software professionals in India is about 15% the average rate in the US. Even though the growth rate of Indian wages is much faster than those in the US, the differential is anticipated to be a source of competitive advantage for many years to come.

Two, the capability of Indian firms to deliver products that consistently satisfy the requirements of clients demanding high quality standards. A NASSCOM analysis of international quality standards of the top 300 Indian software companies showed that 109 had already acquired ISO 900 or SEI certification, and an additional 167 were anticipated to do so by the end of 2000. In fact, Motorola India Electronics Pvt. Ltd. and Wipro Infotech Group were two Indian companies among a handful worldwide to have achieved Level 5 certification of the Capability Maturity Model (CMM) of the Software Engineering Institute at Carnegie Mellon University, a standard that certifies the software development processes within an organization. All these capabilities ensured that companies worldwide recognized India's IT talent and began using it to outsource their software development to Indian companies. Due to the Indian government's efforts to spend significant capital on developing resources for telephone and data communications, and with the availability of satellite links for data communication, the factors that had proved to be a roadblock in the development of this sector in the early 1990s, had more or less disappeared by 1998.

The US firms had the added advantage of a 9.5–12.5 hour time differential between India (Indian Standard Time is + 5.5, i.e. five and a half hours ahead of GMT). So, the US allowed work to be carried out by Indian teams on a 24-hour basis, shortening cycle times and improving productivity and service quality. By 1999, there were more than 626 companies in India engaged in the business of software exports. Of these companies, more than 73 had export revenues in excess of Rs 100 million, as compared to only 5 companies a few years earlier. As many as 41 companies had exports beyond Rs 500 million in 1997-98, a sure sign of the high proliferation and all-round growth of software exports.

The major software companies in India were Tata Infotech, WIPRO, Satyam, NIIT, Tata Consultancy Services, Infosys, and Mastek. The top 20 companies made up over 61% of total software exports. Most of the top 6 companies, except for ITL, concentrated on areas of specialization within the products and services they offered. The largest of these companies, Tata Consultancy Services, operated almost exclusively by providing on-site services to customers across the world, while most of the others had a mix of on-site and offshore development in their business models. It was time for Infosys to decide which way it should go.

Strategy is about setting yourself apart from the
competition. It's not a matter of being better at
what you do — it's a matter of being
different at what you do.

— Michael Porter —

# 12

# A BUSINESS STRATEGY

Narayana Murthy knew the path he wanted Infosys to take — the one that led upward. His vision, from the very start, had been and would remain the creation of wealth for all stakeholders; the only way that could happen was through rapid growth of the organization.

And grow, Infosys certainly did. During the 14-year span from 1993 to 2007, the share issue price of the company increased 3000 times! An investment of Rs 9,500 (100 shares at an issue price of Rs 95) in the initial public offering of Infosys in 1993 (Rs 9,500 was approximately $300 according to the  exchange rate at the time) would be worth Rs 29,440,000 ($665,235 according to the 2007 exchange rate) after adjusting for stock splits and bonuses. This does not include the dividends paid out by the company.

The company saw growth not only in its finances, but in the range of clients that it served. There is scarcely an industry that has not benefited from the professional expertise of Infosys' employees. The list of such industries includes the following:

- Aerospace and Automobile
- Banking & Capital Markets
- Communication Service Providers
- Resources, Energy & Utilities
- Hi Tech & Discrete Manufacturing
- Insurance, Healthcare & Life Sciences
- Media and Entertainment
- Product Lifecycle and Engineering Solutions
- Retail, Distribution & CPG
- Transportation & Services
- Independent Validation Solutions — provides software testing services
- IT Infrastructure Management Services — manages core networks, data centres and servers of clients.
- Real Estate
- Life Science

In addition to these, there are business units aligned to clients' geographies, such as EMEA (Europe, Middle East & Africa), APAC (Asia-Pacific) and CAND (Canada). Infosys also has horizontal business units, such as Enterprise Solutions (ES), which specializes in Enterprise Resource Planning (ERP) and package implementation and works with clients across industries and geographies; Systems Integration (SI), which provides integration services to clients.

However, all this did not occur overnight. The developments took place in stages over years, especially from 1993 onwards.

In February 1993, Infosys conducted an Initial Public Offering (IPO) on the Indian stock exchange with its issue priced at Rs 95 per share but was able to raise only Rs 131 million from it. Most of the investors in the IPO were foreigners, the chief reason being that Indians, by and large, were wary of placing bets on a company that was not part of the big family groups that dominated the Indian business environment. The result was that Infosys became more aware of the importance of investor relations than most companies. 'What we have done in investor relations transcends what we've done in software,' claims Nilekani.

This issue was followed by a private placement of Rs 250 million in October 1994 with institutional investors. Infosys used the proceeds from these issues to expand its operations in Bangalore. Having acquired land from the State of Karnataka in Bangalore, the company built a 160,000 square foot campus on five acres in a Software Technology Park in Electronics City and made it its headquarters. This prism-shaped structure is not merely a striking piece of architecture in the city, its inhabitants and corporate culture are of a standard and nature that has caught the attention of the world.

The year 1999 was a milestone year for Infosys. This year Infosys earned $100 million for the first time and was also listed on NASDAQ. Infosys was the first Indian company to be listed on NASDAQ. In the same year Infosys received CMM level 5 certificate from Software Engineering Institute (SEI).

The booming economy, following the reforms announced by the Indian government in 1991, encouraged various states to provide incentives to companies to locate in their areas. The government made land available to companies on a long-term rent-free lease that automatically transferred ownership to the company after 25 years, provided the land was used for the purposes specified.

Infosys took full advantage of this situation and, over the next few years, established a number of offices around the country and the world. It had its worldwide sales headquarters in Fremont, California, with branch sales offices in Atlanta, Bangalore, Boston, Chennai, Chicago, Dallas, Detroit, Frankfurt, London, Los Angeles, Mumbai, New Delhi, New York, Seattle, Tokyo, and Toronto. A large number of these offices were small leased facilities that carried an option to expand as required. In addition, the company had established software development and training facilities in Bangalore, Bhubaneshwar, Chennai, Mangalore, and Pune to meet the needs of its customers and employees.

Towards the end of the 1980s, Infosys could see the big picture very clearly — in order to survive and grow, it had to get into international business. It also realized the need to draft a clear business strategy so that it could successfully act against threats from competitors and meet the challenges of operating on a global basis. This is exactly what it formulated in the early 1990s.

At this point in time, there were many companies that had sprung up to take advantage of the growing global demand for software development services. Various multinational companies, such as Citicorp, Texas Instruments, Digital Equipment, Hewlett Packard, and IBM had a good mind to fulfil this demand themselves and began to set up operations through subsidiaries and joint ventures. Bangalore was a popular choice for their headquarters chiefly because skilled labour was relatively cheap and the time difference between India and the US guaranteed a 24-hour work cycle on joint development projects.

Murthy's observation was this: 'We felt that in a few years only the fittest will survive. A maturing and polarization of the industry was coming that would separate the men from the boys — global players from the also-rans. It was time to formulate a clear strategy for Infosys that would ensure that it remained a global player for many years to come.'

The strategy that Infosys formulated contained five main elements.

It was the firm belief of the Infosys management that for the company to succeed, one of the most critical factors was a commitment to adhere to high quality standards in all aspects of its business. The company decided that it would differentiate its services by strictly keeping to highly evolved processes, including a detailed approach to planning and execution, multi-level testing, and careful tracking and analysis of quality control. There was a department of quality control and assurance established under K. Dinesh. A Quality and Productivity Charter outlining the aspirations of the company was drawn up, and every employee was given a laminated copy that they could carry with them.

Infosys aggressively pursued the strategy of 'zero-defect' tolerance and achieved ISO 9000 certification in 1993 and Level 4 CMM in 1997. This was no mean achievement in 1997, considering that a mere 2% out of the more than 1,000 software companies tested worldwide had managed to reach this level. Hardly a company to rest on its laurels, Infosys moved ahead to become one of the first Indian companies to adopt US GAAP reporting in fiscal 1995 and quarterly audited Indian financial statements in fiscal 1998.

The management was aware that if Infosys were to continue to be successful, they had to keep working on and honing the ability to recruit, train, deploy, and retain highly talented IT professionals. As Raghavan once remarked, 'Our assets walk out of our buildings every evening...we have to get them to come back! The work atmosphere at Infosys is an incentive for our employees to stay with us. The Human Resources Department focuses on the cream of Indian analytical talent and selects candidates based on analytic ability and "learnability". We have gone from being just another company to a "day-one" recruiting company at the nation's top schools.' (A "day-one" company is a company that recruits on the first day of the recruiting season thereby gaining an edge over other firms.) What Infosys went on to do was to create a campus-like environment, so that new recruits would feel comfortable in a collegial atmosphere and informal culture. This in turn would promote their entrepreneurial spirit and encourage them to give free flow to their ideas.'

Infosys was also the first Indian organization to highlight the importance of its human resource capital and brand equity by equating it with a value in its balance sheet. 'While the value of our human resources for fiscal 1997 is placed at Rs 2,785.5 million, brand value is pegged at Rs 1,728.3 million. Cumulatively, the value of intangibles is Rs 4,513.8 million, which is four times the value of our tangible assets,' observed Murthy. Corresponding numbers for fiscal 1998 indicate that Infosys values its human resources at Rs 5,090 million and its brand name at Rs 5033 million, giving it a total value of intangibles of Rs 10,123 million!

From day one, Infosys had been dedicated to providing managed software solutions, mostly on a fixed-price, fixed-time frame basis. It could give its clients the advantage of receiving high-quality, cost-effective solutions at lower risk by assuming full project management responsibility on every assignment. At the same time, the company realized that if it wanted to protect its margins in the long term, it would have to move from low value-added areas like on-site programming to more highly valued services like IT consulting and product development. Therefore, it began to move into the area of packaged software solutions to address customers' common requests. Gradually, it successfully established a brand of bank automation solutions known as Banks 2000. As Nilekani rationalizes, 'Indian companies are seen as good constructors.... The perception is that given a problem we could easily write a program to solve it. On the other hand, firms like Arthur Andersen and Deloitte and Touche are hired early in the process and paid a premium because they are perceived to have a better grasp of the business. The trouble is that we seem to be brought in after the major decisions are made.'

To overcome this last minor hurdle, Infosys began to deliver high-quality, cost-effective solutions that went even beyond the customers' expectations, relying on the underlying principle that a satisfied customer leads to a successful company. In this manner it created a reputation that encouraged most of its customers to come back to Infosys for repeat transactions.

Over a period of time and through a close scrutiny of its business, the management realized that one of the major reasons contributing to the competitive advantage of Infosys was its access to low-cost engineering talent in India. However, it hardly made sense to make this talent travel long distances to perform work on-site over short periods. Besides, the exorbitant costs involved in such movement more or less negated any cost savings that the company could pass on to its customers. As always, thinking solutions, the company made several significant investments in infrastructure so that it could manage and execute projects at multiple locations in an integrated manner. Well aware that the foremost requirement was to establish its credibility in the market amongst its customers, Infosys took on its first project on-site and established customer confidence in its ability to produce quality, problem-free work. Once it had established this credibility, customers had no qualms about the offshore concept, in the face of the fact that Infosys had the procedures in place to ensure continuous quality monitoring as determined by its Level 4 status in CMM.

Offshore development provided Infosys with a number of advantages. It allowed increased flexibility in allocation of resources. The uncertainty associated with the need to obtain visas and documentation for programming staff to travel abroad was now far less. Customers were happy because they received more cost advantages and Infosys was satisfied because it could make more profit. Thanks to the time difference between India and the US, it took minimal time to address problems — a problem communicated in the evening could be resolved by morning. Perhaps the biggest advantage of an offshore model was that it prevented the loss of key human assets to the global marketplace. Countries like India face the danger of a 'brain drain' of talent because foreign corporations recruit so many of their technical personnel from here.

By 1998, Infosys was able to successfully execute over 80% of its project work in India and at the same time maintain high levels of customer satisfaction. The company had eleven development centres in India which it planned to expand considerably for it had already established a global presence.

This was the last element introduced as part of Infosys' strategy. The company believed that there were four fundamental tenets of a well-run business, namely: predictability, sustainability of predictions, profitability, and a good 'de-risking' model. The common thread running through all these principles is an aversion to surprises of any kind. At Infosys, 'de-risking' implies limiting its exposure to businesses of various kinds. This strategy was not off-the-cuff; rather, it was a result of the company's historical experience. In 1995, GE had accounted for over 20% of Infosys' revenues and 8% of its profits. However, when the time came to renew the contract, there was disagreement on both sides regarding the terms and a competitor won the contract. This incident led to Infosys' implementing a prudent customer 'de-risking' strategy so that too much dependence was not placed on any one customer. Another important aspect of this strategy, as exemplified by its response to the Y2K problem, was to ensure that no single business segment accounted for more than 25% of its revenues.

Despite the fact that there was a huge market demand for solutions in this area in the new century, Infosys adopted a more sustainable long-term strategy. It gradually reduced its dependence on these projects so that it was generating less than 15% of revenues from them by early 1999. It adopted strict guidelines for acceptance of clients to meet its overall revenue and profitability goals. For fiscal 1997, fiscal 1998, and the nine months ended December 1998, its largest client accounted for 15.6%, 10.5%, and 6.7%, respectively, of revenues, and its five largest clients accounted for 43.1%, 35.1% and 29.2%, respectively, of revenues. By bringing about this balance, Infosys was able to ensure the diversification of the technology skill set of the company's IT professionals. This was an imperative requirement for the company to become flexible enough to adapt to changing market conditions as well as to attract and retain highly skilled professionals on the lookout for an opportunity to learn new skills.

An environment which calls for perfection is
not likely to be easy. But aiming for it is
always good for progress.

— Thomas J Watson, Jr —

# 13

# THE CORPORATE CULTURE AT INFOSYS

One of India's largest IT companies, Infosys Technologies Limited operates nine development centres in India and has over thirty offices worldwide. Its annual revenues for the fiscal year 2006-2007 exceeded US $3.1 billion and its market capitalization was over US $30 billion. The company and its subsidiaries employ 153,761 professionals (as on December, 2012). It is this colossal workforce that votes Infosys the best employer to work with.

Recruiting, training and retaining so many employees is hardly a cakewalk. So how does Infosys achieve this happy state? The secret lies in its corporate culture, envisioned and nurtured since its very inception. When the company came into being in 1981, its founders wanted certain ground rules defined for the organization to be consistently successful.

Rule 1

Never use corporate resources for personal benefit. No one at Infosys, regardless of which rung of the corporate ladder he/she may happen to be, uses a company car for a personal errand. This certainly reverses the trend of extant Indian business culture, where corporate titans, more often than not, find it hard to draw the boundary line between their work and their personal life. An Infosys employee summed up this policy in these words: 'Frequently in India, corporate officers make personal use of company assets. We, the employees, have to put up with such practices because there is no choice. Nevertheless, such practices lead to a growing alienation and rebellious withdrawal of creative input. That doesn't happen here at Infosys.'

Rule 2

There is a level platform for everyone in the Infosys family. All its stakeholders, whether they are customers, employees, shareholders, vendors, or society, are treated with fairness, honesty, and transparency.

Rule 3

All at Infosys are treated with equal respect. This translates into a host of welfare facilities for the employees and their families. As Murthy reiterates, 'We have always viewed Infosys as a vehicle for creating wealth for our employees.' As a matter of fact, Infosys was the first Indian company to offer low-cost stock options to most of its employees. On the basis of their seniority, over 60% of employees are eligible to receive stock options. With the run-up in its share price, this practice has created many millionaires among the ranks of employees — over 2000-plus dollar millionaires and 20,000-plus rupee millionaires. An unexpected bonus is that employees themselves are now eager to add value to the company so that its stock price continues to appreciate.

'We want our employees to build up capital assets, to be financially independent, and to be proud of where they work,' says Raghavan, who heads the Human Resources function. To realize this goal, Infosys makes substantial no-interest and low-interest loans to its employees, and makes heavy investments to ensure that its five-acre campus is well maintained and landscaped, providing all employees with state-of-the-art technical equipment. In the Indian business environment, where it is usual to see employees sitting behind 486 and even 386 PCs, Infosys employees enjoy the privilege of working on Pentium® computers.

Rule 4

All discussions must be issue-based. The implication of this principle is that important issues are debated fiercely, if necessary, but without degenerating into personality conflicts. While employees are free to disagree with the views of their supervisors and are encouraged to express their ideas, once a decision is reached everyone works towards implementing it to the best of his/her ability.

Murthy and his co-founders were aware that merely outlining a corporate culture and laying down rules was not enough. If they wanted their employees to fit into the corporate culture, many more steps were necessary. To make sure that its employees are one with the corporate culture, Infosys follows a careful recruitment process, selecting individuals who are not only extremely bright but also have the willingness to learn and an attitude that is conducive to teamwork. It recruits from the top 20% of students from the engineering departments of universities. Applicants for jobs at Infosys are administered a series of tests and interviews specifically designed to select only the best.

In 1998, the company received approximately 74,500 job applications, of which it tested 22,483 applicants, interviewed about 6,300 and extended offers to about 2,000. Of these, approximately 1,550 accepted. The recruitment phase over, the company invests heavily in training. There are 14-week training sessions for newly recruited employees, in addition to a variety of 2-week workshops that focus on enhancement of skills. Apart from these, there are continuing education programmes that are administered by a 35-person faculty.

A unique feature of the corporate culture at Infosys is the extent of empowerment it allows its employees. This is unparalleled, not only in India but in most companies worldwide as well. Senior management at Infosys has an 'open door' policy, and it is quite common to see employees discussing their issues and concerns with them. The seating arrangements also encourage such sharing. Most employees sit in cubicles, with managers' cubicles in close proximity. This permits a free exchange of ideas and dialogue. Then there are other avenues of involvement, such as a committee of employees that decides the cafeteria menu.

Another unusual feature is the radical means of employee autonomy. Once a manager told six of his staff how much money was available for raises, then he put them in a room and asked them to allocate it among themselves. If they failed to reach a decision, he would make it himself. The employees debated, came up with a sensible, workable solution, not an easy, 'everybody gets the same' compromise, and conveyed it to him. The manager was appreciative of their decision, implemented it and saved precious working hours that would otherwise have gone into first making the decision himself and then defending it. So that others can benefit from such practices, Infosys now has an internal 'best practices' forum so that all managers can see how to use for their own needs the successful methods other managers have developed. It is these policies that help Infosys retain most of its employees, while many other organizations struggle with managing a high employee turnover rate.

All the same, with the expansion of the company, changes are bound to creep in, and not all might be welcome. Some of the senior employees at Infosys do express certain concerns. 'A lot of the new people come directly into senior positions and start to want to change things to their way of working right away,' was a remark made by a twelve-year veteran of Infosys. 'In the old days you joined at a junior position and worked your way up the company ranks, which allowed you to understand how the company operated and what made its culture unique. Today, many of the newer employees coming to senior positions are trying to run their departments as separate entities. This is causing us to move from a company with a single culture to a company with many individual departmental cultures.'

That is the flip side of freedom and empowerment. Nevertheless, while senior management concede that this was true in some instances, it is not unduly worried because a majority of Infosys employees join the company fresh out of university and  are able to imbibe and preserve the culture of the company effectively. Deep down, though, everyone is aware that this issue will prove to be a major challenge with the global expansion of the company and the recruiting of personnel in different countries for their offices.

Individual commitment to a group effort — that
is what makes a team work, a company work,
a society work, a civilization work.

— Vince Lombardi —

14

# A DREAM CAMPUS

Just step into the 160,000 square foot campus of the Software Technology Park in Electronics City (Bangalore) in the state of Karnataka, and you know that you have 'arrived'.

It's impressive, and that is an understatement. Ask Jim Pinto of San Diego, California, who visited this awesome corporate campus. This is how he describes it in an article on Automation.com dated March 2007.

'During a family visit to Bangalore, India, in February 2007 I was invited to Infosys, along with my brother and nephew, both well-known local businessmen. We checked into the Infosys complex via Gate 2, with a security check which included issue of individual photo-ID cards for each visitor.

We met with our five people — technical, marketing and human resources — in one of several well-outfitted conference rooms. The people were motivated and their presentations were good. We were welcomed in the main corporate office building, the same one where Tom Friedman of the N.Y. Times was introduced to this unusual company in a way that impressed him enough to inspire the concept of his bestselling book, The World is Flat. We too saw the impressive multi-media presentation on three giant TV screens in front of us, and below a lighted map of the entire complex which houses some 15,000 people in a vast building complex. Like Tom Friedman, we were impressed.

We were then taken on a tour. I've visited the Microsoft campus in Redmond, WA. and also Google's campus in Mountain View, CA. This was larger and more impressive. Considering that we had just come through overwhelming traffic through the overcrowded highways, the contrast was nothing short of amazing. Here were beautiful streets between several huge, impressively designed buildings in university park-like surroundings.

During the campus tour, we were ferried around in one of several golf-cart-like cars — it was clearly too far to walk. There were several bicycle racks, and employees simply took any available bicycle to ride between buildings. There were swimming pools and tennis courts, set amidst lawns and impeccable landscaping. There were indoor pool tables and exercise machines, with restaurants and ATM machines and banking offices. This was truly the heart of Bangalore's 'Electronic City'. At the end of our visit, we were taken to the company store where we could select any Infosys-logo product as a gift to commemorate our visit.'

The physical structure apart, Jim was equally impressed by his interaction with the Infosys personnel. He shot questions at them in quick succession pertaining to varied subjects — technical, financial, marketing, sales distribution, recruitment, motivation — and was pleasantly surprised at the direct and knowledgeable response. He noticed the confidence in the personnel, who spoke unhesitatingly, without waiting for approval from senior managers. The employees' passion and motivation came across all too clearly.

Infosys takes good care of its employees, down to the minutest detail. The corporate headquarters is equipped with a modern quality day care centre manned by trained teachers, sports facilities like a gymnasium, tennis courts, volleyball and basketball courts, a library, and a fully staffed medical centre. Well aware that the route to a person's heart is often through his palate, Infosys provides a subsidized cafeteria with excellent food. And as if this weren't enough, there are comfortable sleeping facilities so that employees who need to work late to finish a project can get adequate rest. Infosys is not the only company in India offering these benefits to its employees; what makes it stand apart is that the management seem to genuinely care a great deal for their employees.

Indeed, Infosys considers its people its greatest assets and does all that it can to ensure that after they walk out the door every evening, they return refreshed the next morning. No wonder it has repeatedly been voted the 'best' employer.

No enterprise can exist for itself alone. It ministers
to some great need, it performs some great service,
not for itself, but for others... or failing therein, it
ceases to be profitable and ceases to exist.

— Calvin Coolidge —

# 15

# INFOSYS

Infosys has come a long way since it was started in 1981 with seed money of only US$250. It has become one of the leading companies at the international level providing services in consulting, outsourcing and technology. Its services are availed by leading companies of 31 countries. As of 2012, Infosys has 66 offices and 69 development centres all over the world.

The vision of Infosys is to be a 'globally respected corporation' with a mission to build tomorrow's enterprise. The values which drive Infosys are summed up in CLIFE which stands for client value, leadership by example, integrity and transparency, fairness, and excellence. Client value is to consistently go beyond client's expectations; leadership by example is to set standards in business and transactions and set example for the industry. Infosys aims to achieve integrity and transparency by being ethical, sincere and open in all transactions. Fairness means to earn respect and trust by being objective and transaction-oriented. Infosys constantly tries to bring improvement in its processes, services, products, employees and become the best in the industry.

Infosys is the pioneer of the Global Delivery System (GDS) which is based on the principle that work should be taken to the place where the best talent is available at the most economical price with the least risk. To help its client companies use their resources efficiently and derive the measurable business value, Infosys follows three processes: transform, optimize, and innovate.

Infosys follows the best-practice process, IMPACT, to deliver value to its clients. It ensures a clear line of sight from process change to bottom-line impact so that the client receives the promised business value. It focuses on delivering on time and within budget to optimize the core operations of the client. This optimization brings efficiency and frees up resources to undertake transformation and innovation. Infosys's lab network, Infosys Labs, has 600 researchers constantly trying to enhance the innovation capability of Infosys so that it remains updated on the latest technology and utilizes it to provide the best solutions to its clients.

Infosys has implemented various measures to reduce its carbon footprint and become an environment-friendly company: its new buildings adhere to the Leadership in Energy and Environmental Design (LEED) standard; its development centres in Hyderabad, Manglore, Mysore, and Pune harvest rain water; its sustainable infrastructure is 25% more efficient than global energy efficiency standards. Infosys used 48 million units of green power across its campuses in fiscal 2012. In the same year it planted 500 trees. Infosys introduced the first commercial radiant cooled building in India and was among the top 10 green companies in the 'Green Rankings 2011' by Newsweek.

The global character of Infosys is reflected in its workforce which comprises of employees from 89 nationalities working from more than 30 countries. 34.7% of its workforce are women. This diverse workforce brings different perspectives and helps develop innovative ideas. Infosys encourages a culture of inclusivity where employees focus on their commonalities to form teams which provide best service to its customers. Infosys was the first Indian IT company to set up an office for diversity and inclusivity which conducts various diversity and inclusivity programmes and constantly tries to motivate its employees to collaborate and innovate.

Infosys educates its employees about values and cultural ethos through live events, mailers, posters and company intranet. The company helps its employees achieve work-life balance through family enrichment programmes and workshops. The volunteer network spread across its seven campuses provides counselling to fellow employees on personal problems. The company also employs persons of different gender identities and provides a safe and respectful working environment for them through its IGLU (Infosys Gay Lesbian employees and You) programme which creates awareness and encourages inclusion. The company provides equal opportunities to the differently-abled people and ensures that they can access the company infrastructure easily.

The IWIN (Infosys Women's Inclusivity Network) is aimed at making the work environment friendly for women employees and grooming them for leadership roles. Infosys encourages its employees to work for community welfare, environment sustainability and digital literacy. The employees can take a sabbatical to work on community development projects of six months to one year duration; the company also provides them monetary support. The Green Connect programme of Infosys encourages employees to work for eco-friendly environment.

Infosys also works for social welfare in USA through its USA Foundation. It gave a grant of US$380,000 for the science education initiative of the New York Academy of Sciences. This programme, named STEM Mentoring Programme, provides mentoring to students from the underprivileged communities of New York and New Jersey in science, technology, engineering and maths (STEM). The after-school programme develops a community of science educators and connects these educators and their students to scientists and their research.

# Infosys - Milestones

## 2012

- Listed on the NYSE market
- Infosys acquires Lodestone Holding AG, a leading management consultancy based in Switzerland
- Forbes ranks Infosys among the world's most innovative companies
- Infosys among top 25 performers in Caring for Climate Initiative
- Infosys crosses the US$ 7 billion revenue mark

## 2011

- N R Narayana Murthy hands over chairmanship to KV Kamath on 19 August
- Infosys crosses US$ 6 billion revenue mark, employee strength grows to over 130,000

## 2010

- Infosys crosses the US$ 5 billion revenue mark

## 2009

- Infosys opens its first development centre in Brazil and second Latin American development centre in Monterrey, Mexico
- Infosys selected as a member of The Global Dow
- Employee strength grows to over 100,000

## 2008

- Infosys crosses revenues of US$ $ 4.18 billion
- Annual net profits cross US$ 1 billion

## 2007

- Infosys crosses revenues of US$ 3 billion. Employees grow to over 70,000+
- Kris Gopalakrishnan, COO, takes over as CEO. Nandan M. Nilekani is appointed Co-  Chairman of the Board of Directors
- Opens new subsidiary in Latin America
- Reports Q2 revenue of over US$ 1billion

## 2006

- Infosys celebrates 25 years. Revenues cross US$ 2 billion. Employees grow to 50,000+
- N R Narayana Murthy retires from the services of the company on turning 60. The Board of Directors appoints him as an Additional Director. He continues as Chairman and Chief Mentor of Infosys

## 2005

- Records the largest international equity offering of US$ 1 billion from India
- Selected to the Global MAKE Hall of Fame

## 2004

- Revenues reach US$ 1 billion
- Infosys Consulting Inc. is launched

## 2003

- Establishes subsidiaries in China and Australia
- Expands operations in Pune and China, and sets up a development centre in Thiruvananthapuram

## 2002

- Touches revenues of US$ 500 million
- Nandan M. Nilekani takes over as CEO from N R Narayana Murthy, who is appointed Chairman and Chief Mentor
- Opens offices in the Netherlands, Singapore and Switzerland
- Sponsors secondary ADS offering
- Infosys and the Wharton School of the University of Pennsylvania set up The Wharton Infosys Business Transformation Awards (WIBTA)
- Launches Progeon, offering business process outsourcing services

## 2001

- Touches revenues of US$ 400 million. Opens offices in UAE and Argentina, and a development centre in Japan

- N R Narayana Murthy is rated among Time magazine/CNN's 25 most influential businessmen in the world
- Infosys is rated as the Best Employer by Business World/Hewitt

## 2000

- Touches revenues of US$ 200 million
- Opens offices in France and Hong Kong, a global development centre in Canada and UK, and three development centres in the US
- Re-launches Banks 2000, the universal banking solution from Infosys, as Finacle™

## 1999

- Touches revenues of US$ 100 million. Listed on NASDAQ
- Infosys becomes the 21st company in the world to achieve a CMM Level 5 certification
- Opens offices in Germany, Sweden, Belgium, Australia, and two development centres in the US
- Infosys Business Consulting Services is launched

## 1998

- Starts Enterprise Solutions (packaged applications) practice

**1997**

- Opens an office in Toronto, Canada
- Infosys is assessed at CMM Level 4

**1996**

- The Infosys Foundation is established

**1995**

- Opens first European office in the UK and global development centres in Toronto and Mangalore. Sets up e-Business practice

**1994**

- Moves corporate headquarters to Electronic City, Bangalore. Opens a development centre at Fremont

**1993**

- Introduces Employee Stock Options (ESOP) programme
- Acquires ISO 9001/TickIT certification
- Goes public

**1987**

- Opens first international office in Boston, US

1983

- Relocates corporate headquarters to Bangalore

1981

- Infosys is established by N R Narayana Murthy and six engineers in Pune, India, with an initial capital of US$ 250
- Signs up its first client, Data Basics Corporation, in New York

# Awards and Honours
# Won by Infosys

## 2012

- Infosys identified as an innovation leader in India in KPMG's 2012 Global Technology Innovation Survey
- Infosys ranked first in the IT Services & Software sector

## 2011

- Infosys Wins 2011 Global Most Admired Knowledge Enterprises (MAKE) Award — the first and only Indian company to win the award eight times
- Infosys wins Platinum Award in The Asset Corporate 2010 Awards
- Forrester names Infosys a Leader in IT Infrastructure Outsourcing
- Infosys chosen India's best company for corporate governance by Asiamoney poll
- Infosys chosen India's most respected company by Businessworld
- Infosys, the most preferred company to work for in India: Business Today survey

## 2010

- Infosys ranked among the top ten value-creating technology and telecommunications companies by The Boston Consulting Group

- Infosys  voted the best company in management, corporate governance, investor relations, and corporate social responsibility (India) in a FinanceAsia magazine survey
- Infosys BPO wins the 'Most Dynamically Developing BPO Centre in Poland' award from Forbes magazine
- Infosys BPO wins 'BPO Organization of the Year' and 'Fun at Work' awards from Stars of the Industry
- Infosys, the most sought-after company in India: Business Today Survey
- Infosys wins American Society for Training & Development (ASTD) award for excellence in inclusivity

## 2009

- Infosys listed on Forbes' Asian Fabulous 50 for the fourth consecutive year
- Infosys ranked among the greenest brands in India
- Infosys in 'India's Best Companies to Work For': Survey by Great Place to Work® Institute
- Infosys in Fortune's 100 fastest-growing companies
- Infosys, the most admired Indian company: Wall Street Journal survey
- Infosys, the Best Outsourcing Partner: Waters Rankings 2009

## 2008

- Infosys BPO wins the Global Six Sigma award

- Infosys wins the NASSCOM gender inclusivity award

2007

- Infosys becomes the first Indian company to win Nielsen Norman Group's Intranet Design Annual Award
- Infosys in Fortune's Top 10 Companies for Leaders
- Infosys Named 'Best Outsourcing Partner' in Waters Rankings Survey

2006

- The most admired company for the 6th consecutive survey by Asia Wall Street Journal
- The Best Company to work for in India 2006 according to the BT-Mercer-TNS survey published by Business Today
- Infosys in Business Week's 'Ten to Watch' companies
- Infosys added to the NASDAQ-100 Index
- Infosys ranked the Businessworld Most Respected Company in a survey
- Infosys one of 74 Global High Performers chosen from Forbes' Global 2000 list
- The Infosys Global Education Centre in Mysore called the 'Taj Mahal of training centres' by Fortune magazine

2005

- Infosys named India's Best Managed Company based

on a study conducted by Business Today and A.T. Kearney

## 2004

- Infosys won the Golden Peacock National Quality Award for 2004
- BusinessWeek ranks Infosys among the top 3 IT Services Companies in the world
- ComputerWorld ranks Infosys among 'The 100 best places to work for in the U.S. in IT'

## 2003

- Ranked as the Best Managed Company in India by Asiamoney
- Ranked No.1 among Asia's Leading Companies in India by Far Eastern Economic Review
- Rated the Most Globally Competitive Company, Most Dynamic Company, Most Ethical Company and Best IT Company by Businessworld
- A Financial Times-PwC survey listed Infosys among 50 companies that demonstrate the most integrity

## 2002

- Ranked No.1 in the 'Best Employers in India 2002' survey conducted by Hewitt Associates for the second consecutive year.
- Golden Peacock Award for Excellence in Corporate

Governance in the Global Category by the World Council for Corporate Governance, London

## 2001

- Infosys ranked number one among the most respected companies in India by the BusinessWorld-IMRB Survey. Infosys was also ranked number one on 13 of the 18 parameters judged by the survey

## 2000

- Voted India's Best Managed Company four years in a row (1996, 1997, 1998 and 1999) by the Asiamoney poll
- Infosys selected as one of Asia's Leading Companies in the Far Eastern Economic Review's REVIEW 200 Survey. Selected as one of the top 10 companies in India — ranked second in 'Overall Leadership' and first as 'the Company that Others Try to Emulate'
- Infosys voted India's most admired company by The Economic Times Survey of India's Most Admired Companies
- Won the Best Managed Company award (1999) by Asiamoney magazine
- Won the Dataquest IT Pathbreaker award
- Selected as 'Organization with progressive business strategies' by the World Strategy Forum
- Featured in Forbes magazine's list of 20 most promising small companies in the world

- Received the IETE Corporate Award for Performance Excellence in Electronics, Telecommunications and IT Industry for the year 1999 from Institution of Electronics & Telecommunication Engineers

## 1998

- Ranked first in the 'Award for Corporate Excellence', The Economic Times, India

## 1997

- Infosys judged one of India's most remarkable and rapidly-growing entrepreneurial companies by the World Economic Forum
- Infosys won the 'Best Regional Company' Award, Bangalore Stock Exchange

## 1996

- Won the Special Award for Excellence under the category 'Innovation of new products', Electronics and Computer Software Export Promotion Council, New Delhi

The sole meaning of life
is to serve humanity.

— Leo Tolstoy —

# 16

# THE INFOSYS FOUNDATION

Hailing from a large family of eleven, the values of sharing and sacrifice for the common good were ingrained in Narayana Murthy from early childhood. Strongly nurtured by the love, value system and personal example of his parents, Murthy continued to be fired with a passion for socialism in the prime of his youth. This zeal to give was doubly reinforced after marriage, for his spouse Sudha thought exactly on the same lines.

Murthy truly believes that '…the real power of money is the power to give it away.' Wife Sudha, similarly, has always believed in JRD Tata's statement: 'If you make lots of money you must give it back to society as you have received so much from it.' She once quoted from the Thatthareya Upanishad, urging her audience that, after looking after their family's needs, they should keep aside one portion of their income for a national institution and another for the poor. At the same time, she is clear that philanthropy should not make the recipients helpless; instead, it should urge them to stand more firmly on their own feet. Sudha says, '…draw a line at what you need. Take your partner's consent. See that you do not make the receiver your dependent. Give as naturally as you eat, sleep or breathe... .Compassion doesn't mean tears and talk....It is not holding meetings and getting your name in the papers.'

The couple is well aware of the magnitude of work required to be done in the social sphere. Once, addressing students at IIT Mumbai, Murthy stated, 'A vast majority still does not have freedom from hunger, from disease and from illiteracy. Our adult literacy is only 58%. 26% of the population lives below the poverty line. 24% of Indians are undernourished. We have been ranked 127th out of 175 nations in the human development index. Clearly my young friends, we have a long way to go.'

On another occasion, he emphasized, 'One of my strongest beliefs is that corporations have an important duty to contribute to society. While, on average, tremendous progress has been made in enhancing the economic well-being of people, the chasm between the haves and the have-nots of the world has unfortunately widened, especially in the developing world. No corporation can sustain its progress unless it makes a difference to its context. Nevertheless, these initiatives should come from the corporation itself rather than being foisted upon by outside parties.'

It was recognition of this need that led to the creation of the Infosys Foundation in Karnataka in 1996, as a not-for-profit trust. The Foundation Trustees comprise Sudha Murthy, Sudha Gopalakrishnan and Srinath Batni. Though both Murthy and Sudha together founded the Infosys Foundation, it actually is the brainchild of Sudha Murthy. The inspiration for this were the parting words of JRD Tata when she went to say goodbye to him after resigning from her job at Telco, when JRD Tata advised her, 'We must give back the profit to the society from which we make it.' This advice had stayed with her. Another incident impelled Sudha  to act on this advice. Her fifteen year old daughter Akshata would read out to some blind students in her spare time. These students could not study further as their families did not have the money to finance their education. One of them wanted to go to Delhi  to study. Akshata asked her mother if she could help that student. At first, Sudha did not give attention to her daughter's suggestion but when Akshata pointed out that despite being capable of helping somebody in need she was not doing so, it forced Sudha to act.

She resigned from her job as the Head of the Department of computer science department of a college of Bangalore University. She told Narayana Murthy that she wanted  to establish an organization to help the needy. Murthy also wanted to do something similar and readily agreed. In 1996, she started the Infosys Foundation, a not-for-profit organization, which has since then been working in the fields of education, healthcare, and social development. The Foundation also establishes homes for the destitute. Since its inception Sudha Murthy has been the Chairperson and trustee of Infosys Foundation.

The operating principle of Infosys Foundation is: 'Bahujana hithaya, bahujana sukhaya' — for the benefit of many, for the happiness of many.  The primary aim of the Foundation is to improve health, education and basic facilities, benefiting a large number of individuals and institutions. It also works in the areas of social rehabilitation, rural uplift, arts and culture. Since its inception, the Foundation has spread to Tamil Nadu, Andhra Pradesh, Maharashtra, Odisha and Punjab. It follows the Build-Operate-Transfer (BOT) model of project financing to develop self-sustainable communities.

The entire Murthy family — Narayana, Sudha, daughter Akshata and son Rohan — have given grants to the Infosys Foundation to the tune of three crore rupees.

Infosys has also instituted social programmes that target educational institutions, specifically in the rural areas. In 1998-1999 and 1999-2000, projects funded by the Foundation included constructing an orphanage, hospital wards, classrooms and a science centre, providing hospital equipment and ambulances, school books, and ancient Indian music cassettes and recorders. By April 1999 the Foundation had committed a sum of Rs 17,337,000 (about US$ 435,000) for projects in Karnataka.

Monetary assistance apart, the Foundation has undertaken innumerable projects on the ground. The following list gives a fair idea of its wide reach and area of work.

- Construction of accommodation facilities for relatives and attendants of patients at the Kidwai Cancer Institute, Bangalore

- Funding the Infosys Super-specialty Hospital for the poor at Sassoon Hospital, Pune

- Installation of office management software at the KEM Hospital, Mumbai for automation of store requirements, accounts and publication of hospital papers and related information on the Web

- Financing the expansion of the Swami Sivananda Centenary Charitable Hospital at Tirunelveli, Tamil Nadu

- Financing the construction of additional blocks at the Bangalore Diabetic Hospital

- Financing the construction of a paediatric hospital for the poor at the Capitol Hospital, Bhubaneswar

- Annual distribution of sewing machines at Bangalore and Sedam (Karnataka) and Chennai (Tamil Nadu)

- Conducting tailoring classes and providing free material to the above prior to giving machines

- Extensive relief activities in: the tsunami-affected areas of Tamil Nadu and the Andaman Islands; earthquake-affected regions of Kutch; cyclone-devastated areas of Odisha; malnutrition-prone tribal areas of Kalahandi

(Odisha); drought-hit areas of Andhra Pradesh

- Establishment of counselling centres for rehabilitation of marginalized devadasis (temple dancers) in north India

- Joining hands with the Red Cross Society to supply free equipment to the rural physically challenged and weaker economic sections of Karnataka

- Monetary aid to the Divine Life Society in Uttaranchal for senior citizens and the destitute

- Donation of books under its 'Library for Every Rural School' project in Karnataka, Andhra Pradesh, Odisha and Kerala

- Publication and distribution of a simple book on computer education in Hindi, Tamil and Telegu for rural students

- Setting up of libraries with books prescribed for hi-tech streams like medicine and engineering in Hubli and Bangalore for underprivileged students

- Donation of an index Braille printer to the Sharada Devi Andhara Vikasa in Shimoga, Karnataka

- Facilitation of education of slum children in Maharashtra, Tamil Nadu and Odisha

- Collaboration  with the Centre for Environment Education for orientation of teachers specializing in science and environment

- Regular assistance for promotion of artistes — underprivileged writers, painters, poets musicians — in rural areas of Karnataka and Andhra Pradesh

- Help for revival of traditional crafts of weavers of Pochampalli, Andhra Pradesh
- Sponsoring art exhibitions and performing arts programmes in Dharwad and Bangalore
- Donating personal computers to schools and the Delhi Library
- Construction of toilets at a school in Pune
- Donation of money for the payment of salaries of teachers
- Assistance to abandoned domestic maids—sponsored airfare from Bahrain to India
- Rehabilitation of street children in Delhi through 'Sathi', an NGO
- Financial assistance to orphanages and schools for the differently-abled in Karnataka, Maharashtra, and Tamil Nadu
- Providing training to tribal communities of Odisha in agriculture, horticulture, sericulture, floriculture, bee-keeping, fishing, dairy, poultry, welding, and carpentry.
- Improvement of rehabilitation centre for mentally-challenged women in Chennai.

Infosys today has marked its presence in India and across the globe in more ways than one. At this juncture Murthy, its Chairman Emeritus, has a few words of wisdom: 'When, one day, you have made your mark on the world, remember that we are all temporary custodians of the wealth we generate, whether it be financial, intellectual, or emotional…I believe that we have all at some time eaten the fruit from trees that we did not plant. In the fullness of time, when it is our turn to give, it behoves us in turn to plant gardens that we might never eat the fruit of, which will largely benefit generations to come. This is our sacred responsibility.'

The Foundation has a holistic view of the betterment of life of all individuals, which is aptly described by Narayana Murthy in these words: 'It is becoming obvious that the world is becoming increasingly interlinked and interdependent, and that we have to collectively move forward. The ever increasing income disparities cannot be neglected. A person is no more an isolated entity and in addition to self-welfare must shoulder responsibilities for society-at-large. One should be trustworthy with all in one's dealings. It is on such foundations that great organizations are created. In the end, unless we can wipe the tears from the eyes of every poor man, woman and child on this planet, I do not think any of our lives is a worthy one.'

The trouble with retirement is that
you never get a day off.

— Abe Lemons —

# Epilogue

Narayana Murthy retired as CEO of Infosys in 2002 and assumed the role of its Chairman and Chief Mentor. According to the regulations of Infosys, the Chairman's retirement age is 60. Therefore, Murthy retired as Chairman of Infosys in August, 2006 and remained its Chief Mentor till 2011. Since then he is the Chairman Emeritus of Infosys.

After his retirement from Infosys on 19 August, 2011 as its Chief Mentor, Narayana Murthy continues to have a vision for the future. What Infosys did for middle-class India, he is trying to do for the country's poor with his venture capital fund, Catamaran, set up in 2009 after he sold part of his and Sudha's shares in Infosys.

His life continues to be nearly as hectic as it was during the three decades he spent nurturing the company, the drive that spurred him on not having faded at all. In an interview with The Indian Express in September 2011, he said, 'I am one of the hardest working people I know.' He also denies any intention to join politics.

'I am not seeking a position. I have no desire for a bungalow or a car…Prime Minister Atal Bihari Vajpayee invited me to join his cabinet in 1999. But I was running the Infosys marathon at the time. I told him I still had a lot of work to do and respectfully declined.

India faces many challenges today. Foremost is whether we will be able to sustain the fruits of liberalization that we were fortunate enough to receive in the last 20 years, whether we will be able to create a just and equitable society, whether we can leave a better India for our kids who are worried about corruption, and worried about inaction.

I am an Indian first. Whatever has been asked of me by my country, I have discharged to the best of my ability. I am not seeking office. And anyway, one person is not sufficient to raise the confidence of 1.2 billion Indians. We need thousands of inspirational leaders in every sphere of life.

The solution is not for a 65-year old to become a rookie in politics. The opportunities need to go to modern, energetic young people. People like me can play an advisory role. There is an opportunity to create an advisory council for the country. But who am I to wish this? I don't have experience in public office. It is perhaps presumptuous of me to suggest this.'

He still travels for the major part of each month for meetings as he is a member of the United Nations Foundation, Ford Foundation and the Rhodes Trust, of which he is a trustee, and when he is in Bangalore, he arrives at his office at 9 am sharp. Though he no longer participates in strategic or tactical issues at Infosys, his protégés still call him up for advice and he continues interacting with and inspiring Infoscions worldwide.

# Journey Through the Years

| | |
|---|---|
| 1946 | Narayana Murthy born on 20 August in Mysore, Karnataka |
| 1967 | Completed Bachelor of Engineering from Mysore University |
| 1969 | Completed M.Tech from IIT Kanpur<br>Joined IIM Ahmedabad as Chief System Programmer |
| 1972 | Moved to France to join SESA company |
| 1975 | Joined System Research Institute started by an IIM Ahmedabad professor in Pune |
| 1977 | Joined Patni Computer Systems in Pune |
| 1978 | Married Sudha Kulkarni |
| 1981 | Co-founded Infosys Consultant Pvt.Limited with six friends in Pune |
| 1983 | Infosys office shifted to Banglore |
| 1992 | Infosys renamed Infosys Technologies Limited |
| 1993 | Infosys issued first IPO<br>Infosys received ISO 9001 |
| 1995 | Inauguration of Infosys Software Park in Banglore |
| 1996 | Infosys Foundation started |
| 1999 | Infosys earned $100 million for the first time<br>Infosys listed on NASDAQ<br>Infosys received Capability Maturity Model (CMM) level 5 quality certificate from Software Engineering Institute |
| 2002 | Murthy stepped down as CEO, became Chairman and Chief Mentor of Infosys |
| 2006 | Retired as Chairman, became non-executive Chairman, continued as Chief Mentor |
| 2009 | Venture capital fund Catamaran started |
| 2011 | Retired as non-executive Chairman and Chief Mentor, became Chairman Emeritus |

# Awards Won by Narayana Murthy

1996       IT Man of the Year by Dataquest

1996-97   JRD Tata Corporate Leadership Award

1998       Distinguished Alumnus Award by IIT Kanpur
          Star of Asia by Business Week for three
          consecutive years (1998–2000)

1999       Emerging Markets CEO of the Year  award
          by Emerging Markets and ING Bearings
          Businessman of the Year award by Business India
          Electronic Man of the Year Award by Electronic
          Industries Association

2000       Padma Shri by Government of India

2000-01   Businessperson of the Year award by The
          Economic Times

2001       Wharton Business School Dean's Medal by
          University of Pennysylvania
          Max Schmidheiny Freedom Prize by Switzerland

2002       Asia's Businessman of the Year by Fortune
          magazine
          Ernst & Young Entrepreneur Of The Year

2003       World Entrepreneur of the Year award by Ernst
          & Young, first Indian to win
          Indo-French Forum Medal by Indo-French
          Forum, first recipient

2005       Included among the ten most admired global
          business leaders by The Economist

2007       Commander of the Order of the British Empire
          (CBE) by Government of UK
          Lifetime Achievement Award by The Economic
          Times

2008       Officer of the Legion of Honour by
          Government of France
          Padma Vibhushan by Government of India

2009       Woodrow Wilson Award for Corporate

Citizenship by Woodrow Wilson International Centre for Scholars, USA

2010    IEEE Honorary Membership by Institute of Electrical and Electronics Engineers

NDTV Profit's Lifetime Achievement Award

2012    Chosen among '12 greatest entrepreneurs of our time' by Fortune magazine

Hoover Medal for philanthropic activities in India

Recipient of The James C. Morgan Global Humanitarian Award by The Tech Museum, California

Narayana Murthy has 25 honorary doctorates from universities in India and abroad

❑❑❑

Printed in the USA
CPSIA information can be obtained
at www.ICGtesting.com
CBHW021429231124
17916CB00011B/305